LIFTING

THE VEIL

Beloved Dead, Biography &
Other Appreciations

MAX EHRMANN

Edited and Introduced

By Tim Dalgleish

DEDICATION

To 'Wunni' for all her kindnesses, conversation and love

CONTENTS

ACKNOWLEDGEMENTS

DePauw University Archives and its library staff in Greencastle, Indiana, deserve my sincere thanks and appreciation for all their efforts on my part. They were always swift and positive in their responses to my requests and never stinted on giving me the help I needed. I would like to thank specifically, Wes Wilson, the Coordinator of Archives and Special Collections, who was especially kind and helpful and his colleague, Archives Researcher, Taylor Zartman.

I also have to thank my wife Sarah for, as ever, looking the text over and for slowing me down.

INTRODUCTION

On August 27th 2010, a life-size bronze sculpture by Bill Wolfe was unveiled at the corner of Wabash Avenue and North Seventh Street in Terre Haute, Indiana. The figure depicted is of a man, neatly but casually dressed in a suit and tie, sitting on a bench. His legs are crossed, one arm is draped across the back of the bench. The other arm rests on his knee, he has a pencil and pad resting there. He looks thoughtfully off into the distance. The face is wistful, stern, philosophical. This busy corner was a favorite spot of Max Ehrmann's, whom the sculpture embodies. Scattered at his feet, on brass plaques on the floor, are quotes from his most famous work, the prose-poem *Desiderata*, written in 1927 when Ehrmann was in his mid-fifties.

The intersection, on this corner of U.S. Highway 40 (the old National Road) and U.S. Highway 41, was once called *'the crossroads of America'*. Designated, the year before Ehrmann wrote *Desiderata*, as part of the Federal Highway system, U.S. 40 was the gateway to the West and dreams of new settlements. Terre Haute, like Ehrmann, once lay at

1

the heart of things. Although his hometown has not forgotten Max Ehrmann, many in the world of literature have.

In researching the materials for this book, I decided to look through the archives of that venerable literary publication *The New York Review of Books*. I assumed, there would be a few articles on this author, who in his time was the friend, acquaintance or correspondent of the likes of Nobel Laureate Sinclair Lewis, the novelist Jack London, Theodore Dreiser (author of the classic *An American Tragedy*), Eugene V. Debs (the union leader and founder of the Industrial Workers of the World or 'Wobblies'), Havelock Ellis (the physician and social reformer who put sexuality on the map in the nineteen-thirties), Birth Control campaigner, Margaret Sanger, the radical editor and political activist, Max Eastman, Booth Tarkington, author of *The Magnificent Ambersons* and many other notable figures. However, Ehrmann's stock has fallen so low in the literary world since his death in 1945, that to my surprise I could find nothing on him in *The New York Review of Books* (which was founded in 1963).

This apparent amnesia is curious but has happened before with Ehrmann. One Sunday during Lent in

1956, Reverend Frederick W. Kates, the rector of Old St Paul's in Baltimore, placed on the pews, as was his habit, a poem. The poem, mimeographed onto sheets with the parish letterhead, was *Desiderata*. Perhaps because it was only a little over a decade since Ehrmann's death and the rector assumed his congregation was familiar with the text, or simply because he relayed it in his sermon, either way, Reverend Kates failed to include the name of the poem's author on the handout itself. The letterhead simply read *'Old St. Paul's Church, A.D., 1692'*.

An alternative version of the story has it that Ehrmann's name was omitted by a member of the congregation when passing it onto friends. Either way, copies of the poem slowly began to leach into the local community and eventually into the consciousness of the burgeoning youth movement, nascent, but growing across America at that time. Hippies, Flower Power and the 'swinging' sixties, saw the poem reproduced on posters and in underground magazines, misattributed, however, with the urban myth, *'Anonymous, written in 1692, found on a plaque on the wall of Old St. Paul's Church'* and so on.

Not until 1965, with the death of Adlai Stevenson,

the former Democratic presidential candidate and US Ambassador to the United Nations, did the issue of authorship come to national prominence. Stevenson died in London, on July 14th, during a stop-over back from Switzerland. Soon after, a column by Betty Beale appeared in the *Washington News* and was syndicated nationally. In her column, she was objecting to a cover story in *Time* magazine, which had claimed that Stevenson was a lonely and gloomy figure. This Beale rejected, reporting that his close friends said otherwise. In support of her argument, she wrote,

'When he took off for Geneva [shortly before his death] he left behind on the bedside table in his New York apartment a printed page that he had marked. Perhaps it was intended for a commencement address [others have said he intended to use it in his Christmas cards that year]. He did not write it but that he chose it and saved it for his attention upon his return is indicative of his own thought. It was entitled Desiderata, *and it was originally found in Old St. Paul's church, Baltimore, dated 1692.'*

In her next column Beale corrected the error and named Ehrmann as the poem's author but perhaps unsurprisingly, in some quarters, the 'Anonymous' authorship of this piece of supposed 17th Century Americana continued being promulgated. Indeed,

1968 saw *Star Treks'* Leonard Nimoy release an LP with his rendition of the poem included but re-titled *Spock's Thoughts*. Not to be outdone, in 1970, *Bonanza's* Lorne Greene read it on the *Johnny Cash Show*, as did Joan Crawford, in the same year, on David Frost's TV show. Then in 1971, Les Crane, a former talk show host, recorded the poem. Crane was accompanied by a musical arrangement from Fred Werner which included a gospel choir and harpsichord. This reached number 8 on the *Billboard* charts and went on to win a Grammy for Spoken Word Recording in 1972. In 1978 Richard Burton recorded it as part of a *'personal anthology'* entitled *The Hound of Heaven*. Max Ehrmann's name didn't appear on any of these TV shows or recordings, and the verse was usually misattributed. A typically ironic example of attribution was the credit given on the Les Crane LP, which read, *'Produced by Fred Werner and Les Crane for Old St. Paul Productions.'*

In the age of the internet, Ehrmann is now generally credited with authorship of the poem, but he still remains a shadowy figure on the literary stage. Aside from *Desiderata* most of his work remains unknown. *Lifting the Veil* is perhaps one of his most obscure pieces, but deserves to be better known, as it reveals much about the philosophy or weltanschauung of the man behind *Desiderata*.

Lifting the Veil was published in the June 1927 edition of *The Harvard Graduates' Magazine*, a worthy but not widely distributed publication. As far as I know, the essay has not been published since and certainly not in book form. With a poet's passion and a scientist's precision, Ehrmann endeavoured in the essay to go beyond the efforts, as he would have put it, of the philosophers of the ages. This sounds very grandiloquent and as his nephew Winston W. Ehrmann reminisced, in his early days Max saw himself as middle-class Bohemian. In fact, because of his tendency to strike a rather highfalutin, Victorian tone, Ehrmann won a certain kind of immortality (one he wouldn't have appreciated very much) when he and *Desiderata* were ridiculed in another Harvard publication, *National Lampoon*. Parodying the Les Crane version of the poem, the *National Lampoon Radio Dinner* album featured a track called *Deteriorata,* and lyrics such as *'You are a fluke of the universe'* instead of *'You are a child of the universe'*.

Ehrmann would have disliked such parody, not for his own sake, but largely because he felt that the commercial world and popular culture fed off such trivialities. As he saw it in this essay, naïve as it may be, he was attempting to tug gently at the veil of reality and in doing so open up the question of meaning in an often seemingly meaningless world.

In very accessible prose he swiftly outlines Kant's Idealism, the Absolute Idea of Hegel and the *'metaphysical fiction'* of Schopenhauer and the dominance of Will. He also saw himself as pushing beyond the contemporary philosophy of his time, which was epitomized by the English thinker Francis Herbert Bradley and his notion of the 'totality of experience' being God.

In the essay, Ehrmann attempts to combine the superman or übermensch of Nietzsche with the grounded human being of the Natural Sciences, so as to produce a devastating, elemental and spiritual vision which would tap into his contemporaries fears and anxieties. In common with many great thinkers and writers of his time including, for instance, Havelock Ellis, there is a drift toward eugenics in the essay. Eugenics was a term introduced by the half-cousin of Charles Darwin, Francis Galton. Galton sought to co-opt Darwin's evolutionary theory (in a manner Darwin strongly disagreed with) by grafting it onto the notion that desirable human qualities were hereditary traits which could and should be manipulated to produce improved humans.

Such Social Darwinism, if one can call it that, from the nineteen-twenties and thirties (and especially after the rise of Hitler and the Nazis), rightly has a very bad name. Briefly, and without laboring the point, the issues here are tangled and complex and I would direct the reader to John Carey's book, *The Intellectuals and the Masses,* for a flavour of what Ehrmann and his generation were thinking when it came to eugenics. Certainly he was not alone in toying with the idea, as other twentieth-century intellectuals such as W.B. Yeats, H.G. Wells, George Bernard Shaw, Virginia Woolf, E.M. Forster and many others did to a greater or lesser degree. Today it often feels that eugenics was simply an early version (or vision) of modern-day genetics, usually from a basically humanitarian but unfortunately paternalistic perspective, rather than some grand totalitarian or class-based conspiracy out to engineer a modern-day dystopia.

Ehrmann certainly presents his various polemics in dramatic terms in *Lifting the Veil.* If humankind is on the edge of the apocalypse, man-made or otherwise, we can, he feels, go beyond such destruction. If mind and matter are not divisible, incompatible, heterogeneous elements, but essentially the same, cannot, he argues, *'an age of psychological discovery, when mariners, laden with marvelous treasures of thought, return from far voyages in the seas of the soul'* and reveal this unity?

Ehrmann believed passionately in the ongoing evolution of human beings physically, mentally and spiritually. In this essay he distilled eloquently much of the philosophy that lay behind his poetic nature.

In the archives of DePauw University (Ehrmann's small, church-affiliated, alma mater) I came across an early piece of his called *Biography*, a short, five-page manuscript. The neatly written prose is revealing in several ways. As with most of Ehrmann's manuscripts, *Biography* shows little emendation, and I think this is because of his settled views and precise thinking. He was fond of intellectual, scientific and philosophical conversation. He regularly dropped into the nearby Indiana State Teachers College to devour, over lunch, a wide variety of intellectual fare - as half a dozen of its Professors attest in his wife's biography of him, written shortly after his death.

No doubt such regular, academically rigorous talk, helped hone his thoughts on what he was about to write. One can easily imagine him sitting at his desk, in his modest three-room apartment above a printer's shop, as calm and composed as the small figurine of Buddha which he had upon it. Before putting pen to paper, he usually had a very clear idea of what he wanted to write it seems, at least for his non-fiction pieces.

The core of *Biography*, which immediately follows *Lifting the Veil*, is that the writing of biographies is not essentially about what a person *did*, the dates and the facts and figures, but rather about what the person *thought*, their inner life. Greatness, and thus biographical worthiness, was '… *in proportion as [a] life facilitates the manifestation of the worldthought'*. Looked at carefully, this short piece of manuscript prose, is itself, an insight into the inner workings of Max Ehrmann.

Biography is followed by another piece from the DePauw University archive which I've called *'Max's Own Copy: A Short Biography for the Newspapers'*. This is two typed sheets of what appears to be Max's standard response to requests from journalists for information on his background. Written across the top of the first page, possibly by Bertha Pratt King, Max's longtime companion and (in the last few months of his life) wife, *'Max's own copy for papers'* and at the bottom of the second sheet, *'He dictated it on a request'*.

Written before the Second World War, it is very brief (and definitely not a biography of the *'inner life'*) but nonetheless has numerous snippets of interest: he notes an anecdote about his father in the Civil War; his famous professors at Harvard in the intellectually heady days of the 1890s; his energetic days of giving public lectures and his busy article writing during World War I of which he was obviously proud.

Written in 1919, the fourth item in this collection, *Inceptions*, elaborates and expands the notion of the inner life by outlining the five parts or voices which spoke from within Ehrmann himself. *Inceptions* is in the main the imaginary, internal dialogue of a playwright. The playwright is clearly a stand-in for Ehrmann who had, in the previous decade, produced his major trilogy of religious dramas: *The Wife of Marobius, David and Bathsheba* and *Jesus: A Passion Play*. *Inceptions* was appropriately written for *The Drama, A Quarterly Review Devoted to the Drama* where, two years before, J.Vandervoort Sloan had given a good account of these plays saying, *'One feels the author's sincerity, his earnest effort to revitalize the Christ story in terms, not of conventional belief, but of simple human tragedy and simple human faith which looks through the tragedy for the old heart belief and the old heart inspiration, now to so many lost in the religious brocade of doctrine'.*

The five parts in *Inceptions*: the Artist, the Philosopher, the Socialist, the Bourgeois and Little Humour all portray the 'complex' that makes up the playwright (or his understudy Max Ehrmann), each 'character' pulling the complex individual in different directions.

Inceptions is followed by another four essays by three authors and then Sloan's appraisal. Professor Harry V Wann, one of Ehrmann's regular interlocutors (mentioned above), gives us the basics of Ehrmann's publishing history, as does the next essay by Olive Inez Downing but from a more romanticised and laudatory perspective.

Downing, president of *Poet's Corner, Inc*, quotes Elbert Hubbard, a prominent writer, publisher, artist and philosopher of the Arts and Crafts Movement, as saying, *'It looks to be as if Ehrmann is almost the greatest poet in America'.* She stands in Max's office, looking through his books, one feels, more with the awe of a fan than the narrow gaze of the critic.

Two pieces by George Bicknell, written some years apart, note the growth of Ehrmann, from an interesting moral polemicist (a kind of cross between Jesus and Nietzsche) to that of a substantial and noteworthy artist.

To round things off, firstly there is *Beloved Dead*, from one of the many anthologies that included Ehrmann's writing. A lesser known 'mood piece', once spoken by Ehrmann at a funeral service, *Beloved Dead* is an example of something he wrote originally for a *personal* purpose, but which he saw fit to publish because it also spoke to universal feelings found in the wider world. *A Prayer* and *Desiderata* had taken similar paths into print. *A Prayer*, for instance, was a personal reflection written when he was ill. The poem was saved from the wastepaper basket, where Ehrmann had flung it, by his friend Edwin Markham.

The final tidbits are a curio, the *Promotional Comments From 1906 to 1951*, of interest because they show the efforts to which his publishers, the *Dodge Publishing Company* in New York, went in attempting to make him not simply well regarded but popular. As Leigh Eric Schmidt puts it, in his excellent book, *Restless Souls, The Making of American Spirituality* (which has a final chapter on Ehrmann), *Dodge's* assiduous efforts to make him an *'inspirational writer'* of his generation certainly led to *A Prayer* and *Desiderata* entering *'a netherworld of ceaseless reproduction'*. Schmidt is equally perceptive in placing Ehrmann within the tradition of the well-known American nonconformist spiritual thinkers and writers, such as, Thoreau, Emerson, Whitman and James, whilst also noting the lesser known figures of that tradition, such as Sarah Farmer, Rufus M. Jones and Thomas Wentworth Higginson.

Schmidt captures well the author of *Desiderata* and the reason for his place in the tradition when he says, *'Ehrmann held to a spiritual perspective on the world through a mysticism of natural beauty, deep feeling, lonely repose, and resurrected enchantment.'* Ehrmann frequently returned to childhood events, the dreamlike qualities of nature and especially the stirring and inspirational nature of the stars and the cosmic vastness. As Schmidt puts it, '[These] *fleeting moments of awe and serenity kept meaninglessness and alienation from dominating him, though they hardly eliminated his nihilistic suspicions.'*

It should also be mentioned, that tucked into the folds of the various essays are eight of Ehrmann's poems: *A Prayer, A Tradesman and A Poet, Ere You Lie Down to Sleep, Desiderata, The Greater Heroism, The House of Fortune, Love Someone* and *An Artist's Prayer.*

Written on the bronze notebook of the Ehrmann sculpture on Wabash and 7th Street are the words *'Here is the world in miniature'*. These words, written in tribute to his hometown, the place he lived and worked almost his entire life, were the last line of the poem *Terre Haute* and capture the spirit, I hope, of this book.

Here, in miniature, is the world of Max Ehrmann. The various biographical pieces that follow the main essay, and which were written during his lifetime, convey how highly Ehrmann was once regarded in the literary world of North America and, to a lesser degree, Britain. As I indicated, Ehrmann felt biography was not just about names and dates. Nonetheless, included are pieces which err on the factual side of biography, simply because at this stage, the twenty-first-century reader probably still needs a little help in knowing what would once have been common knowledge, at least in the literary circles of Ehrmann's world.

I hope in the future, with this book as a small beginning, that it is not only the facts about Max Ehrmann's life that become better known but also the spirit and philosophy that energised and inspired his work.

LIFTING THE VEIL

by Max Ehrmann

Published in *The Harvard Graduates Magazine*, June 1927

A Turkish cadi, chiding an Englishman for intellectual curiosity, said, *'Will much knowledge create thee a double belly or wilt thou seek Paradise with thine eyes?'* Our answer would have been, *'We crave not a double belly; but we would seek Paradise, if there is one - yes, cadi, even that.'*

In my boyhood, my native city was once placarded with the announcement that, upon a certain evening at one of the theaters, a wonder-man would lift the veil. In a confused, indefinite way, people understood what the announcement meant. It was at a time when the people, almost everywhere, were being given some account of the universe by spiritualists. On this particular evening many persons paid admission, and at eight o'clock were waiting for life and death to be explained by some mysterious performance, they knew not what. There was serious expectancy mingled with humorous curiosity. But the mental cast of the audience as a whole was serious. Sharply at eight o'clock the wonder-man stepped in front of the curtain, and requested the audience, after indulging in ten minutes of the usual

17

theater chatter, to be breathlessly quiet for a time. He promised to open their eyes. Ten minutes passed, and ten minutes more of almost absolute silence. Nothing happened. Five or six minutes more. Still nothing. Murmurs arose, there were shuffling feet and catcalls. Some men climbed up on the stage, went behind the curtain, returned presently, and announced the disappearance of the wonder-man with the box-office receipts. He had indeed *'opened their eyes,'* not to life and death, but to the cupidity of man. In other cities he lifted the veil in like manner, until he found his natural repose in prison; and he died there. If he could return, no doubt now he would make good his former promises, for he has looked behind the veil.

I hope not to leave a like sentiment in the breast of the reader, as this performance unfolds before him. I shall not run away, and there are no box-office receipts. And if I do not actually lift the veil, I shall show something of the mechanics of how, in all likelihood, if lifted at all, it one day will be accomplished.

Man always has wondered at the riddle. At the dawn of history, the riddle was a simple one, *'Who is running the world? And how may we gain his favor?'* The answer that satisfied was likewise simple. All religions have endeavored to answer these questions of the Who and How. It is with these questions that metaphysics and ethics deal. It is with these questions that we are now concerned. What vastly different answers satisfy different persons as to the Who and the How! Often there are thousands of years difference in the answers that satisfy two men confabulating on a street corner. Our quest will be for an answer that shall satisfy him whose culture has discarded the answers that give satisfaction to the primitive minds still among us.

Despite all the philosophical jargon through the ages, not one philosopher has so much as peeped through the veil, that he might tell us what lies beyond. Metaphysical system after system has wrapped up and unwrapped the ghost; and as far as positive knowledge is concerned, man has come from the philosophical clinic no wiser than before.

> *Myself when young did eagerly frequent*
>
> *Doctor and Saint, and heard great argument*
>
> *About it and about: but evermore*
>
> *Come out by the same door where in I went.*

The *'veil'* is a poor figure of speech. The mystery rather lies beyond a wall reaching in height to the Milky Way, and spreading in thickness to the brilliant Capella. Or to make a figure of speech of Einsteinism, - that a ray of light is really a curved line, *'bent light'* - we might scale a million walls a million light-years high, only to return to the abode of ignorance from which we started. We are born, we live, we die, and the gods keep their secret. But will they always keep it? I do not think so, and that is the purport of this excursion in thought.

Few intellectually cheap persons, such as the wonder-man of my native city, practice veil lifting. Let us examine a few of the classic veil lifters. Let us select those whose influence has been so powerful as to color the thinking of Occidental mankind. You see, I am doing what the wonder-man did in my native city years ago, I am asking the audience to wait a little. But we must wash our mental states of the influence of a few of these wonder-men, before we can proceed to point the new way that we believe leads to the back of the veil. Moreover, these famous wonder-men will show us the way that we are not to take in our quest for the answer to the great riddle.

Kant was the greatest metaphysical gymnast of all the ages. His influence still rules much of man's thinking. I propose to tell, in a few words, what was the result of his endeavor to lift the veil. (Dear teachers of philosophy in colleges, do not laugh, or cry out, *What! explain Kant in a few words!*) Kant concluded that man could never lift the veil, never know reality, god; because the human mind gives only falsehoods. The mind is merely a machine for the practical purposes of living. It is like a printing press set up to print the *Morning Times*. As it is set up, it will print that and nothing else. Just so our minds, which are *'set up'* to see and know just this kind of a world and no other kind. And this world we see and know is not real. It is illusion, a show-world, a dream-world; it is manufactured in our own minds. Kant called the thing back of the veil *The-Thing-in-Itself*, but he could not tell what it was. His belief that the world we see and know is a dream-world is still stalking the streets of man's thinking. And here I beg the reader to note that it is just this dream-world, show-world, that Natural Science deals with and supposes to be very real. But of this later.

Hegel said that through the veil he saw the Absolute Idea, the perfect spirit, that had triumphed over all contending ideas. This Absolute Idea was composed, in perfect unity, of all ideas, even including its enemies, which it has mastered. The god Hegel thought he saw is a portrait in whose face we see the final, spiritual triumph; but we see also upon his body the deep scars of all the tragedies of the world that make up that triumph. Also, Hegel thought our world not real as we know it. To him, it was somewhat less, but still, a show-world, a dream-world, somewhat like a stage and scenery, where the supreme Absolute Idea develops and perfects itself. And please remember that it is this world that Natural Science believes not a show-world but a very real world.

The next great philosopher to charm the world with metaphysical fiction was Schopenhauer. He had enthusiastic followers, just as Nietzsche has to-day. He has them still. Men said, and still say, *'Here, at last, is one who has lifted the veil.'* What, then, did Schopenhauer fancy he saw behind the veil? The reply is as encouraging as the knowledge that one's forebears are in a lunatic asylum and that one's self soon will be there. Schopenhauer said that there is no answer to life. Everything in the universe is illusion, nothingness, except force, energy, WILL. There is nothing in the universe but god, and god is a passionate, raging, senseless energy, a WILL. He is in each of us, making mischief for us in this world of illusion. This world, as we know it, with all its color, sound and form, is a mere show-world in which raves this wild beast of the WILL within each of us. One has but to look at the mad outer world of today, and the mad world within one's restless self, and see how near Schopenhauer came to describing life as it actually is. This restless god of senseless WILL is driving mankind at a terrible pace. And all about what? Nothing! Life is a farce in which there is no laugh, a tragedy that has no sense.

Here in Schopenhauer, as in Kant and Hegel, our world, the world of outer things, is supposed to be illusion, a dream-world, a nightmare world, merely a plaything for the senseless idiot WILL to kick and buffet about. That was why Schopenhauer believed in resignation anything to quiet, to soothe, this crazy, passionate energy in each of us. And this united, total energy, this monstrous lunatic god, is what he fancied he saw behind the veil.

One other philosopher, and we shall have done with these endeavours at high class, realistic fiction. (I never should have mentioned them at all, were not the whole atmosphere of man's deep thinking loaded with them. Man's thinking is struggling to shake them off, especially their attitude toward the outer world, the world with which Natural Science deals.) Hegel and Schopenhauer described the god they saw. Bradley describes him much more completely. His book, *Appearance and Reality*, has developed a doctrine of veil lifting that has gathered momentum for thirty years. That is a brief period in philosophy. There is a real charm in this god that Bradley has described. Suppose you could gather together all of your life's experience, and suppose you could gather together the experience of all other minds, past and present, you would know God. He is the totality of all experience. He is a one, a unity. We shall understand this totality of experience, this God, when we enter the immortal life, for then we shall have thrown off this human mind, this machine for the practical purposes of living, this instrument which gives us the outer world as real when in fact it is only illusion. In the immortal life we shall permeate the totality of experience; we shall know it completely; in fact, we shall be it.

Bradley also says that this world out there that we call the real world, is illusion, just as the other philosophers had said. But Bradley was unlike them in that he believes it not all illusion: it has degrees of reality. If you had asked these philosophers, *If nature is unreal how does it get its uniformity? Why does fire always burn and water always run down hill?* they would have replied, *There is no nature at all. What appears to be the uniformity of nature is merely the uniformity of mind. Mind gives nature what uniformity it appears to have. Anyway there is nothing but mind in the universe.* We should remember that Natural Science deals with this very world that these philosophers call unreal, and that Natural Science supposes it to be very real. In the view that we shall take, Natural Science has a right to regard the world as real; and it is along the way of the world that we are about to travel to obtain an answer to life, to lift the veil.

We have disposed of these four philosophers in a shorthand method, which may cause learned gentlemen of the classroom to smile. For a quarter of a century, I have tried to view the landscape of human life through the eyes of these philosophical birds, but it has been with ever increasing conviction that their eyes were spectacled with glasses that belied the facts. In order to find reality, to lift the veil, to obtain the answer to life, in short, to know God, we must abandon the closet of consciousness and embrace the outer world.

For it is on the ladder of this outer world that we are to climb into paradise, if there is one. At least that is our duty now. In some future age of psychological discovery, it may be an equal duty for us to return frequently to the house of consciousness, there to hear alien whispers that travel on no physical medium. But even this return to the inner life in some future time must not be regarded as a denial of the reality of the outer world. But these philosophies deserve study. They are splendid mental gymnastics, they remove superstition, they afford a vaster view of life than the antics of the latest movie hero, and they provoke Natural Science to ever greater and greater endeavor. They are masterpieces of realistic fiction. These philosophers told what they fancied they saw, and they gave their view of the cosmic plot. But they are failures as veil lifters. They offer no evidence which would stand in a court of law, certainly none that could endure the inquisition of a scientific laboratory.

The notion that our world is a show-world, a world of illusion, is fading out. A majority of the younger philosophers do not believe it. They hold that the world we see and know, the world that Natural Science deals with, is a real-world - real as we see and know it.

But what has Natural Science brought us as a veil lifter? What answer does it give to the Why? What? Whither? that croaks unceasingly in the pit of consciousness? Natural Science's answer makes man to shudder and his blood to chill. To look in the face of man's ultimate destiny as thus far revealed by Natural Science is to paralyze hope. Gliding through the vast spaces of the universe, there are millions of dead worlds, on some of which perhaps during eons past there lived passionate folk not unlike ourselves in their eagerness to know, in their ceaseless crying out to the heavens for an answer, in their eagerness to continue to live and love. Now all long since sleeping an eternally unwaking sleep, crushed out in an instant by some cosmic accident, or burned in a world aflame, or frozen by the dwindling fires of a sun, or doomed by what other horrors we know not; all endeavors lifted the veil upon this scene. Perhaps such a doom awaits our earth. And what is man in this picture? He is, of course, nothing. Renan expressed a common opinion of scientists:

It may be that the whole development of the human race is of no more importance than the moss or the lichen which forms around any moist substance.

The utilitarian aspects of Natural Science delight the heart of man automobiles, moving pictures, 'radio,' etc.; but its metaphysics stuns him. Here is another rendering of the same scene by a master craftsman of despair, Anatole France:

One day the last survivor, callous alike to hate and love, will exhale to the unfriendly sky the last human breath. And the globe will go rolling on, bearing with it, through the silent fields of space, the ashes of humanity, the poems of Homer and the august remnants of Greek marble, frozen to its icy surface. No thought will ever again rise toward the infinite from the bosom of this dead world, where the soul had dared so much.

Let us set the stage for our own veil lifting. As stated at the outset, our performance may go awry. If we do not lift the veil, we shall show the mechanics of how it is to be done. Even then nobody will be able to do it, but everybody may help.

If the laws of nature are not the laws of the Reality, of the Ultimate Truth, of God, pray whose are they? These laws are showing how God runs the universe. Natural Science is coming to its own as metaphysics. But what of Anatole France's picture of a few paragraphs back? What of the doom that awaits our globe and all upon it?

Is it necessary to accept such a despairing conclusion? Natural Science has discovered only a hundred thousandth part of the letter A in the alphabet of all possible knowledge about our universe. Ought we not, therefore, to speak modestly when we speak of last things, of the whole truth, of the ultimate truth? Shall we describe the coast of Africa because we have in our hand a pebble from the beach at Mombasa? Are our minds, lately emerged from the jungle, competent to sit in judgment on the destiny of worlds? The truths that Natural Science has revealed ought not thus to be overstrained by us, who are only beginning to learn to think. Another and different interpretation of Natural Science may be just as reasonable as our despair of a few paragraphs back - nay, to the man of the future it may be more reasonable. And to show this shall be in part our task. Of course, mathematical exactitude must not be expected here. Our journey is adrift in the dark.

Would it not be singular if human evolution now ceased? Yet it is the common belief of every age that to it the last word is spoken and in it the last task of the universe completed. Queer vanity! There are those who affirm that man will evolve no more. After having climbed laboriously for millions of years, from the thing that crawls and thinks not at all, to his present status, man will remain unchanged for the remaining hundreds of millions of years, until some other world bumps into us, or we lose our equilibrium by too much or too little accretion and fly into celestial dust, or until the earth becomes thin-blooded and like an old woman sits beside the emberless hearth of the sun, or until man by his scientific *'monkeying'* with powerful forces shall unwittingly burst us asunder, or until some sudden flare-up of the sun burns us to a crisp.

The following figures are compromises from various authorities. After the Pithecanthropus erectus (the walking Ape-man) nature labored 300,000 years to produce the Heidelberg man, and then another 100,000 years to groom the Piltdown man, and still 50,000 years more to fashion the Neanderthal man, and yet another 25,000 years before the Cro-Magnon man, the first true man, appeared. There were still 15,000 years before the morning twilight of history. Staggering figures! Really not so when we consider the age of the earth, probably 100,000,000 years. Not until half that time had elapsed did animal life get itself formed out of plant life. Then another 49,500,000 years were required by animal life to reach the walking Ape-man.

There was considerable change in the physical structure from the Ape-man to the Cro-Magnon man. But it was as nothing compared to the mental change. The senses of these early men were many times keener than ours. But back of the senses, in the inner ranges of the mind, it was a murky twilight world. Hundreds of thousands of years had to elapse before self-consciousness lighted up the darkness, before the man-child learned to say, *'I know that I am,'* before reason became to him a guide. Fancy a Heidelberg man, squatting before his cave, and blinking at the setting of an Early Palaeolithic sun. What could he foresee of the modern schoolboy, in a chemical-physical laboratory, making a spectrum analysis in search of helium in this same sun?

Just as we of to-day are superior to this man-child of hundreds of thousands of years ago, is it not reasonable to believe that our far descendants will be superior to us? The after-man, the superman, will deal with aspects of the universe now unknown to us, by methods equally beyond our mental ken. How is it possible to look at the universal history of man and to say that it has no purpose? Nature has labored through the myriad ages to produce the present man. She will not cease in her endeavor until she has set his feet within the very portals of the gods. This later-man will have as his ally the mechanical contrivances of science. Only one thing can wreck the realization of this vision - man himself.

It is estimated that it took the laborious, tragic and wasteful methods of nature 500,000 years to pass from the Java man to the Cro-Magnon man. How much more quickly will an equal change in man be wrought now, by the swift, painless, and self-conscious method of domestic selection! A change of perhaps equal greatness will be wrought by man upon himself in a hundredth part of that time. Creative biology is entering upon a career hitherto undreamed of. It is not impossible that, in some modified fashion, Professor Haldane's little jest will come true. *'I can foresee,'* says Professor Haldane, *'the election placards of three hundred years hence...* *'Vote for Smith and more musicians,'* *'Vote for O'Leary and more girls,'* *and perhaps finally,* *'Vote for Macpherson and a prehensile tail for your great-grandchildren.''*

Thus far in our little journey we seem to have been more or less in the company of Nietzsche. But the companionship has been negligible. In fact, from now on Nietzsche is our greatest antagonist. Eternal Recurrences stand before the portals of the gods to drive away the superman. (I beg that it be remembered by literal-minded and prosaic persons that 'portals' and 'gods' are figures of speech.) We set out upon a quest for some answer to life. We have proposed to develop the superman, ever more and more, until he shall lift the veil and know the answer, if there is one. If Nietzsche's theory of Eternal Recurrences is true, our journey ends here. If it is only plausible, we must discredit its plausibility. It is a barricade thrown up in the highway we must take, for it hurls the superman down again, whereas for our purpose he must carry on.

Nietzsche would say that there are no portals and gods, literal or figurative. Next, he would say that the superman will have ages and ages of devolution, of going downward, of retracing his steps, back even to the club and the cave and the hairy squatter blinking at the sun. The eternal treadmill theory of human life was common enough before Nietzsche. He greatly vitalized it, and gave it a fresh despair. In *Thus Spake Zarathustra* he says:

Must not everything that can go already have gone down this path? Must not everything that could happen already have happened, and this slow spider that crawls in the moonlight, and this moonlight itself, and I and thou... must we not all have been here already, and borne back, and gone on... Must we not eternally come back?

That is, will not man eternally go up and down the ladder? Or will not this bit of WILL that each person is, re-enter some lower form to begin again the painful process of evolution? and when the superman stage is reached, will it not return again to the ant, and so on up and down, eternally, eternally? In *The Will to Power* Nietzsche gives another account of Eternal Recurrences:

If the universe may be conceived as a definite quantity of energy, as a definite number of centers of energy... it follows that the universe must go through a calculable number of combinations in the great game of chance which constitutes its existence. In infinity, at some moment or other, every possible combination must have been realized... And inasmuch as between every one of these combinations and its next recurrence every other possible combination would necessarily have been undergone, and since every one of these combinations would determine the whole series in the same order, a circular movement of absolutely identical series is thus demonstrated. The universe is, therefore, shown to be a circular movement which has already repeated itself an infinite number of times, and which plays its game for all eternity.

Nietzsche further tells us, in *Thus Spake Zarathustra*, that the world has no ultimate purpose. And in *The Will to Power* he says,

If the movements of the world tended to reach a final state, then that state would already have been reached.

The line of thought hangs well together: if there are Eternal Recurrences, of course there can be no final state. But is not all this only assertion? Are not the facts that touch this problem, however meager, all on the other side? In the case of man upon earth, is there any evidence that he has already traversed every possible state of development? The evidence is rather that he has gone steadily forward; and that if he wills it, he may continue steadily to go forward, perhaps until he rends the veil and receives the answer to life from the very lips of the gods.

What of Nietzsche's statement that *'If the movements of the world tended to reach a final state, then that state would already have been reached'*? Our reply is that in *some portions of the universe that final state may indeed have been reached.* As for us upon earth, all the evidence is that we are still young; and our earth itself is a mere child, as the ages of worlds are reckoned. We have not yet had time to reach a final state. 'Final state' as here used is interpreted as the superman's ability to lift the veil and to read the answer to the riddle. If this is not the final state, it is not far from it. Once having the answer to the riddle of life, we shall be able to live accordingly, that is, to attain to the final state or equilibrium, to be in tune with the universe. Or if there is nothing back of the veil, no answer to the riddle, the knowledge of that fact will spare man henceforth his questioning, and so he will attain another kind of final state.

Nietzsche would say that the fate of our earth is but to repeat the fate of millions of other worlds now sailing noiseless and lifeless the seas of the firmament. And this is the prevalent interpretation of modern science. We have only to recall Anatole France's picture of the last expiring life on our eternal ice-bound earth. This terrible vision already has chilled generations of questioning men.

We are still in the domain of speculation and not in the domain of science. We have as much right to speculate as had Nietzsche and our speculation seems - to us at any rate - to fit better than his the experiences of human life. There is another conjectural reading of Natural Science, and it is this other reading that we are trying to justify.

Will the superman be able to save himself and his world in that day of catastrophe that men predict? Will he preserve the effects of every worthy human endeavor during the countless ages that man shall have trodden the earth? Will he be able to do this, and to persist in his endeavor to lift the veil, until he knows the answer to the riddle? Or will he be crushed to nothingness?

We do not think preposterous the assumption that he will be able to save himself and to learn the answer to the riddle before the day of doom - if indeed there is any such day. His mind will be as superior to our mind as ours is to the Ape-man's. William Herschel's epitaph reads in part, '... *he broke through the barriers of the skies.'* That is what the superman will do.

What marvels have been revealed by mechanical means in the last fifty years! Fifty years? They are as nothing compared to the time units we have been dealing in. With ten thousand years of domestic selection behind him, with ten thousand years of the findings of Natural Science, including psychological discovery, may not this superman in reality lift the veil?

We said at the outset, *We are born, we live, we die; and the gods keep their secret.*' But do they? Have they not already been forced to speak? However reluctant, under the inquisition of test tube and crucible, have they not already been forced to give up some of their secret? Or it may be that our attitude toward the gods has been wrong. They may be crying out to us; but we do not hear their voices; or hearing, we do not understand their language. But we are learning it. And in the millions of years of life still possible to our earth, it may be that we shall learn enough to light other fires when the sun is reduced to embers, or learn how to cool ourselves in some sudden parching flare-up of the sun, or dash to safety should some fellow planet be in our path, or maintain our equilibrium by conscious endeavor should the unequal distribution of cosmic dust among the heavenly bodies rearrange the pull of gravity. Of course one smiles - and rightly at such suggestions. But they are intended to express nothing more definite than a great confidence in the superman. The Ape-man must often have grinned as some brother made wild suggestions; and we are the Ape-man of that superman who may not feel us even in his bones. Today we do things with nature that no enlightened person or the last century, if told, could possibly have believed in. Just so our descendants will perform what to us would be miracles, what in our state of knowledge simply cannot be done. Surely no great degree of imagination is required to see that this is true; but there is always that feeling of silly finality about the present which invariably declares itself to be the last word.

And moreover, these final catastrophes may be but nightmares; or if they happen at all, it may be long after our descendants have looked behind the veil, read the answer, and have safely deposited man's contribution in some spiritual world. These predictions of catastrophe have not the certainty of a chemical formula. Take, as an instance, *'the sudden excessive flare-up of the sun,'* which would burn us all to death. We know that there are suns that do this, rising temporarily from low magnitudes to first and second magnitudes. Why may not our sun one day do likewise, parching us as corn cast into a fire? Indeed we know that our sun has these flare-ups on a small scale. The answer is that a sun that flares up probably does it periodically, and in consequence its planets have not the time between flare-ups to develop superior living organisms, if indeed any kind of living organism. A sun that does not flare-up periodically probably does not flare-up at all, and such it may be is our sun. No one knows what destiny awaits our earth. What conclusions we have are only conjectures built upon sparse data. The future may give more comforting knowledge. We are feeling our way in the twilight. The superman will walk in the light.

The trail we have been following thus far lies in a real world, a world of trees and stars and planets and peoples, spreading through vast spaces that are likewise real. It is unlike the world of the idealistic philosophers, whose world was merely consciousness. Our world is one on which we can work toward the great end.

Our view is not materialistic, for it includes consciousness as well as matter; nor is it idealistic, for it includes matter as well as consciousness. The world is not reducible wholly to matter or to mind. Both may be real as we know them. Both may be real to the gods just as they are real to us. And we may one day understand a closer kinship between them than now appears. Physicists and psychologists are investigating. Matter is appearing more and more clearly to be energy; and energy and mind do not seem to be as far apart as matter and mind. Physicists and psychologists may bridge the chasm. Meantime we will accept hope and help from both matter and mind, for in our view they are the same thing. In accepting help from mind we do not, as did our idealistic philosophers, discredit matter.

Therefore some future cosmophone, whose messages ride a yet-to-be discovered medium, may one day reach a thought-world, spirit-world, in whose keeping are the good and the beautiful that man has cherished.

Let us assume that our faith in the superman's ability to save his material world as we know it is a foolish faith. Let it be assumed that the physical world as we know it is doomed. Docs this end the story? There is another and different aspect connected with this desire to lift the veil. It considers man's purely mental life. The horizon of the superman's inner life, his psychical life, may reach into distances that touch the very confines of other vaster thought-entities. May there not be an age of psychological discovery, when mariners, laden with marvelous treasures of thought, return from far voyages in the seas of the soul? May not the superman, on the far margins of his inner life, one day hear the music and understand the language of other thought-worlds? To describe this we must speak in symbols, for we are still in a mental prison; but the superman may roam a universe in the limitless areas of his soul. He may find other and higher planes of consciousness, from which to view not only the vaster panorama of the outer world, but also the vaster panorama of his own soul, which is somehow but narrowly separated from all souls. And in this panorama of his own soul he may find spiritual kinships and connections. We, in our day, only glimpse these other planes of consciousness. Most of them we designate as abnormal. The superman may live quite naturally and healthfully in a different mental world, whose suns and stars never yet once have lighted up the dark labyrinths of our souls. In these psychical wanderings he may enter vast cities of thought, wherein are preserved the forms of the marbles of the Greeks, the songs of all the Homers, and every good and beautiful thing, and every love that craved to live eternally its day of earthly bliss. What matter, then, if the physical world be doomed? In these wanderings of the spirit, the superman may learn the answer to the riddle.

Have we here surrendered our thesis, the thesis that in a real material world, on the ladder of Natural Science, we shall climb to the paths of the gods? When just now we contemplated the destruction or the physical world, and when we spoke of *'spirit-world'* and *'thought world'* as remaining, did we in fright run back into the arms or the idealistic philosophers, the philosophers we tried to discredit at the outset of our journey? We think not. For we believe that it is still in a real material world that the superman is to seek this *'spirit-world,'* this *'thought-world.'* Also, when we spoke of the destruction of the material world, we spoke of its destruction as we know it, not of its annihilation. Moreover, with us, matter and thought are not incompatible, heterogeneous elements. They are the same; and we have faith that science will close the gap between them. And, finally, at the outset we denounced the idealistic philosophers not for their belief in a world of thought or spirit, but for their disbelief in the reality of the material world.

We can no more truthfully say that we have reached the end of man's evolution than could the Ape-man truthfully have said that he himself had reached that end. The truth is rather that we have reached but the real beginning. We are only now marking the direction of the trail that leads into the midst of the far distant future, where we fancy and hope are the portals of the gods. And nothing but man himself can prevent the making of this map, and the traveling of this road. If man's quest of the gods and the answer to life be a holy one, surely everything that aids that end is virtue, and what retards it is sin.

42

BIOGRAPHY

By Max Ehrmann

Unpublished manuscript from the DePauw University Archives

Having become at times satiated with imaginative reading and having been carried far distant from the usual course of men by idealism and socialistic dreams, I have turned for help to reality. Not to history, but to biography. History cannot teach me how to conduct my life, for it deals with nations. It is the conduct of nations in their collective relations toward each other and themselves. I have turned, therefore, to biography. *How have other men lived?* It is true that all men are alike. There is a common ground which all traverse. There is childhood and parental influence, youth and prevalent public opinions, manhood and struggle, maturity and influence (great or small), decay and death. Therefore biography can teach me in those things which all men have in common. It furnishes a total view of life, how one period grows out of another, the causes of thought and temperament and the consequence of actions.

Submerged in petty concerns, it is this total view of life that we need; or lost in a sea of dreams, it is this history of real men and real conditions that will call us back to actual life.

The exact date and place of a man's birth and the thousand little circumstances of his life can have no great value in biography except as they show his inner being. What a man thinks, why he thinks it, his ideals of life and the motives of his need no less than his deeds – these are the essence of biography. There are biographies that are accurate enough about dates and places, but the *life* is that of the biographer: *his* motives and passions masquerade in the subject's attire. A biographer should be a man of broad experience. This requires struggle with men and the variety of emotions that result from failure, success, suspense, hardships, wealth, poverty, health, sickness etc., requires genuine, not play experience. How can one describe emotions which he has not felt? Every man sees as many kinds of men in the world as he himself has been.

The biographer is not an advocate. From the dust and ashes of the past, it is his task to bring back a departed soul with hopes, fears, ideals and motives all its own. He is the artist of the inner world, who is a very different person from the artist of the outer.

Some biographies are like outlines that drawing teachers place before beginners: one may fill them out with whatever of the stuff of the inner life that he chooses. And one may be assured that the reader will put his own life into the unfilled place. Such biographies can teach nothing other than dates, and they of themselves are worth almost nothing.

In a manner, the world seems always to have understood itself. It has acted like one man, and not like fragments. As a whole, its process has been slow and silent. To think that it changes quickly is to be ignorant of causes. Great human noises are manifestations in different quarters of change that has already come. And the world works on in silence while a portion of humanity cry out in their private anguish. No man has got the world dissatisfied with itself, moved it on, or turned it over. No man makes the world's history, but the world makes every man's history. Those persons who think that great men make history, fail to see the background that made them possible, and of which they are only the spokesman and servants.

The mission of great men has been to understand the thoughts of the world mind and to interpret and proclaim them in words, deeds or art. 'World mind' is not a figure of speech. Every man thinks about different things; but all men have similar thoughts. The total of all men's thoughts is no chaos, but a system, a unity. Great men are those who tell us in words, deeds, or art the nature of this unity and the nature, strength, and direction of thoughts that compose it.

Every great man is so because of some definite service. We all see and understand his work now, but in his generation perhaps men did not believe him when he said that it was the trend of the world mind. And history has sustained him; he saw what there was that other men could not see. *But what he saw was.* Amid the trillion thoughts of men, he saw what was in the air and caught the direction of the wind. Sometimes when yet afar off, he understood the forming of world thoughts, and bade men prepare. Sometimes he has told men more about themselves than they knew, as in art. He is a reader in the invisible book which is the basis of all men's thinking.

A man is great in proportion as his life facilitates the manifestation of the world thought.

Whose voice whispered to the great man the *thoughts* that *the world* was having? Amid the teeming minds and many voices that entered his consciousness how did he know which came direct from men's souls and would outlive all others and give character to all subsequent history? That portion of a great man's life which shows this secret revelation is the very heart of biography. In what attitude did the great, indomitable, irresistible thought of the world mind of his day, whose servant he was to be, and which was to give him immortality, first appear to him – how did he know it – in what way was he persuaded – what held him in its thraldom – how did he view his relation to his apparent duty – was the struggle tragic – did he go like a willing son to obey his father's voice – or did he resist until he could no longer withhold from following the light – in his heart, did he believe himself to be following his own or the light of God – was it a conscious or unconscious process – if it was a conscious process, why did he chose this method rather than that; if unconscious, what accident brought it to pass - did he know the importance of the work he was doing? These dissenting elements showing his relation to his world work are the chief duty of biography. They are not easily done, but they are the aims at which biography ought to strive.

'MAX'S OWN COPY'

A Short Biography for the Newspapers

By Max Ehrmann

Unpublished from the DePauw University Archives

Max Ehrmann was born on North 4th Street in Terre Haute. The house still stands. When he was a little boy, the family moved to 638 North Center. Max Ehrmann's father was a railroad man. During the Civil War, he built railroad bridges. He was once under enemy fire and shot [at] from a bridge. For twenty-two years after the close of the Civil War, he worked for the Vandalia (now Pennsylvania) Railroad. Later he with his oldest son, Charles Ehrmann, engaged in the coal business with mines at Ehrmanndale, Indiana. It was in this coal office on Ohio Street that Max Ehrmann worked in for five years.

His father and mother, being Methodists, sent him to DePauw University. They were members of the German Methodist Church. The original building still stands on Mulberry Street between 4th and 5th. At DePauw Ehrmann edited the *De Pauw Weekly* and was president of the Northern Division of his fraternity,

Delta Tau Delta. After graduating from DePauw, he entered the postgraduate school of philosophy at Harvard University.

Among his teachers were the now famous professors James, Royce, Palmer, Munsterberg and Santayana. At Harvard Ehrmann edited *The Rainbow*, the official national magazine of his fraternity. On returning to Harvard, Ehrmann studied law, was admitted to the bar and was deputy District Attorney of Vigo County for one term. Later he was tendered the nomination for State Senate but declined. He canvassed the district for his party on several occasions.

He became seriously ill and went to Colombia, South Carolina to recuperate. Ill, lonely, and far from home, he wrote *A Prayer. A Prayer* has been published into millions of copies – legitimate and pirated. It is known to have been translated into thirty-two languages and dialects. Returning from South Carolina, he went to work for the *Ehrmann Manufacturing Company*, owned by his brothers. There he worked ten years.

During these years Mr Ehrmann gave public readings. The first was at St. Mary's of the Woods [College, Terre Haute] and the last, twelve years later, during author's week, at Vandervoort Music Hall, St. Louis. Mr Ehrmann gave up readings because he had contracted an infection of the throat. This happened while giving a poem at the dedication of a monument in southern Indiana over the grave of Sarah Lincoln, Abraham Lincoln's sister. There was an immense crowd, and he strained his voice.

During the World War, he wrote many war articles, enough to make a book. These articles were gathered together and are now in the State House in Indianapolis. Recently, on the one-hundredth anniversary of DePauw University, Mr Ehrmann's *De Pauw University Cenntenial Ode* was read. DePauw University conferred on him the degree of Doctor of Letters. Mr Ehrmann's books and booklets are as follows: [not included here].

INCEPTIONS

A Footnote to the Psychology of Play Writing

By Max Ehrmann

The Drama, A Quarterly Review, May 1919

In each one of us there is a multitude of attitudes, points of view, poses, personalities. Every debate in the congress of the soul reveals how manifold we are. Voices that frighten us break into the debate, voices we never knew had a seat in our governing house, voices from the cellars of consciousness, and voices coming suddenly from behind the doors of mysterious committee rooms, voices of crime, and voices of love. Sooner or later, in the midst of the debate, one voice receives the support of the will. That domineering personality shuts off debate with a ruthless hand. This is not a congress in which the majority rules. The will may become enamored of the most timid of all the voices, one scarcely heard amid the combat of words; and backing its cause, will carry it triumphantly through, often in the face of prudence, honor, success, wealth, and every other member of the congress of the soul. How did the timid voice charm him? By what mysterious art of lobbying did it win the will's support? What went on behind closed doors, that is, behind consciousness?

We are a machine that is free, which is, of course, a contradiction.

There come times when an author must try to fly again, to take a long journey in the imagination, that is, to begin another book. He may be moved by the needs of his family, or by a hunger less material in himself. In this new flight, he may hope to catch the vision of some new form of beauty, to sweep the sky for grains of spirit gold, for some new glint of gilded sun or painted cloud, for an air-route, it may be, to the brotherhood of man.

His mind is turned into a parliament house, and within him there begins a debate. Certain personalities purporting to represent him, open a discussion as to what kind of book he should write. The author really seems to have nothing to say upon the question under discussion. The gentlemen inside him are fighting it out. He merely sits listening in the gallery of himself:

ARTIST: Write something beautiful.

PHILOSOPHER: Make the people think.

SOCIALIST: Write something that will teach economic justice.

BOURGEOIS: Bah! Write something that will pay.

ARTIST: We shall write something beautiful to place beside our other books. You all remember, during the writing of these books, how I handled the wheel and took you on some wonderful flights.

SOCIALIST: Not one of these books touched the one big problem of life - the economic problem. As gilded moonshine, they were well done.

BOURGEOIS: And they never paid much.

PHILOSOPHER: Their reward was of the spirit.

BOURGEOIS: Nonsense! One cannot live on that. Now listen to me. Why not write something with thought in it, but not over the people's heads; something about industrial conditions, but not anarchy; something with beauty, but not too much; and something with a lot of good fun in it? Such a piece would 'go' at the box office.

PHILOSOPHER: You mean a play?

BOURGEOIS: A ripping play!

ARTIST: Ripping?

BOURGEOIS: A cross between The Importance of Being Earnest *and* Hedda Gabler.

ARTIST: It would be a monstrosity.

BOURGEOIS: For a play to succeed it must be almost farce, as well as near tragedy, and it must have philosophy of the forward-looking brand, and it must be modern. It has got to give all the thrills for one price of admission.

ARTIST: No thing of beauty can be all these in one. No play can be great art and be modern. Modern life is ugly and lacks unity. Ancient life was, in reality, just the same. But we imagine it was different. We conceive of ancient life as having been beautiful and harmonious, like Greek things in stone. We see ancient life through a charmed veil, through an idealized dream; and that is the setting necessary for great art. A kitchen scene with the odor of cooking vegetables, or a wholesale grocer asleep at the opera, are not subjects for art. What is the use of writing about life as it is? We have it all around us as it is, more minutely done than any artist can do it, in all its ugliness and lack of form and unity. I suggest we do one of the old things, the story of Amnon and Tamar. It is beautiful, and it might be made a vehicle for the love rights of women.

BOURGEOIS: We are not thinking of pleasing the critics. We want to please the people. It's the people that pay. Think! Can't someone think of something?

PHILOSOPHER: Here is a plot: A socialist becomes rich by gambling at the stock exchange and by semi-criminal 'jobs.' He soothes his conscience by the thought that his method is the same as that of all capitalists. In proportion as his success grows, he abandons socialism and becomes capitalistic in his convictions. He has a beautiful daughter who is a true socialist, and ignorant of the source of her father's wealth. The father's principal victim is a capitalist, who has a fine son. The girl's father, now turned capitalist, ruins the capitalist, who turns socialist. The beautiful daughter of the former socialist taught socialism to the fine son of the former capitalist. Finally the crooked father of the girl is discovered, and the 'stolen' wealth is returned to the father of the son, who again becomes a capitalist, and the father of the girl is wrecked. He again becomes a socialist. At the very last he says, 'Because a socialist has stolen is no argument against socialism.' *But he doesn't have to go to prison. The fine son of the former victim, the capitalist, saves him. The whole thing must be sprinkled with fun and sound sense. Of course, the young people marry, the fine son of the capitalist and the beautiful daughter of the socialist.*

BOURGEOIS: *Great!*

ARTIST: *I do not see anything for me in this.*

BOURGEOIS: *You can color the sunsets, touch up with silver a moonlight or two, or gild a grief. After it's done the whole thing will need to be varnished a little, but not too much! We don't want this to be literature.*

ARTIST: *You talk flippantly about art.*

PHILOSOPHER: *I shall have to carry the principal burden. And we have very little humor.*

LITTLE HUMOR: *Gentlemen, I know I am weak. But by the aid of the study of Wilde things I might become strong.*

PHILOSOPHER: *It is pitiful.*

BOURGEOIS: *It is pitiful.*

SOCIALIST: *Yes, it is pitiful.*

ARTIST: *Yes, it is very pitiful.*

BOURGEOIS: *I'll market the play when it's done.*

ARTIST: *I don't think much of your marketing of the other plays.*

BOURGEOIS: I did the best I could. Your painting is well done, but it wants perspective. It wants toning, and only time can do it.

ARTIST: You talk as if I were only a painter. I make music, as well. And I give form to things, including your chaotic twaddle.

PHILOSOPHER: Gentlemen!

SOCIALIST: Confine yourself to the point under discussion. Going back to the fundamental problem of the economic conception of history...

And so on and on, for hours, for weeks and months, it may be. In these days Bourgeois, Socialist and Artist are likely to be prominent members of every author's private congress. One grows very tired merely sitting listening in the gallery of one's self. Suddenly will rushes in and takes a hand.

Philostratus relates in his *Life of Apollonius of Tyana*, 'On one occasion Euxenus asked Apollonius why so noble a thinker as he and one who was master of a diction so fine and nervous did not write a book. Apollonius replied, "I have not yet kept silent." ' Not long thereafter he began his period of silent meditation, which lasted five years. Five years speaking not a word, but listening every waking hour to the debate within the parliament house of his own consciousness, before he felt he might trust himself to be worthy of so great an enterprise as the writing of a book!

O Man of Tyana, would that thy voice might be heard in these days of haste, when writers are concerned mainly with quantity and the love adventures of characters whose heads are packed with sawdust!

MAX EHRMANN – THE POET

by Harry V. Wann

Being part of a program entitled Max Ehrmann: A Recognition. *Given at The Sheldon Swope Art Gallery, Terre Haute, Indiana, the afternoon of Sunday, June 24th, 1945, at 3 pm.*

Lovers of poetry, lovers of beauty in all its forms:

Max Ehrmann was born in Terre Haute and has spent most of his life here, except for the period of his college and university training and for brief sojourns elsewhere. This must be because he has been happy here. Unlike many of the city's illustrious sons and daughters who have forsaken her, he, almost alone among her better-known literary progeny, has remained faithful to her. It should be a source of pride to us that he has chosen so to do.

Mr Ehrmann was graduated from Depauw University where he had edited the college paper. He then spent two years in graduate work at Harvard University, where he studied under the now famous quartet of James, Royce, Palmer and Munsterberg, and edited the *Rainbow*, national magazine of the Delta Tau Delta fraternity. In 1898 his first work was published, a collection of stories and sketches called *A Farrago*. He practised law for several years and was deputy prosecuting Attorney for one term. He became well known locally, and later nationally, as a liberal thinker and reformer, but declined in 1898 the nomination for State Senator.

Already he preferred the quiet, contemplative life.

The Mystery of Madeline Le Blanc, which he describes as a *'Creeper'*, was published in 1900. He would not write it again, says Max, and adds, *'But would any author write any of his books again?'* *A Fearsome Riddle* was published in 1901, as well as a play called *The Animals*, which was unsuccessful.

In 1903 *A Prayer* was published. With the tremendous popularity of this outpouring of his heart in a time of illness and depression, far from home, you Terre Hauteans are familiar. You knew it, and you knew Max before I came to this city. Enormous publicity accrued to it from the fact that a framed copy was stolen from the Indiana Building at the World's Fair in St. Louis. Shortly after, the volume entitled *A Prayer and Selections* was published. *A Prayer* was printed in the Congressional Record in 1909. In 1908, Judge Terry B. Crane of the Court of Special Sessions gave a copy to every person convicted in his court. *A Prayer* has been translated into thirty-four languages and dialects. It is known all over the world. Millions of copies have been sold. Many, many copies have been distributed to our wounded soldiers during the war. Its impact upon the spiritual life of men and women of all races and creeds and in all walks of life defies any attempt to estimate it.

In 1904 *Breaking Home Ties* appeared. It was set to music in Berlin, and for a number of years formed part of Mr Ehrmann's readings on the Lyceum platform. In 1906 came a volume of *Max Ehrmann's Poems*, followed in 1907 by *Who Entereth Here*, a collection of poems. Another collection appeared in 1910. It was in September of that year that he was invited to join the Author's Club in London.

From this time on, Max gave his entire time to his literary work. In 1911 he published *The Wife of Marobius*, a play dealing with physical versus spiritual love, and which he considers the most chaste in form of all his books. In 1913 he wrote, among other things, an extremely radical sonnet entitled *The Congress*. It was widely reproduced.

In 1915 came *Jesus, A Passion Play*, which has been deservedly reprinted a number of times. Especially noteworthy is the starkly realist trial of Jesus before Pontius Pilate.

The author has succeeded better than most of those who have attempted it, in recreating the atmosphere of Biblical times, as we imagine them to have been.

During the first World War, Max Ehrmann wrote many articles and poems in support of the war effort. His *Portrait of the Kaiser* was widely copied in newspapers.

The play *David and Bathsheba* was published in 1917. Here again, the author has succeeded remarkably well in recapturing, the spirit of Biblical times. Vandervoort Sloan called it his finest achievement up to that time.

Mr Ehrmann gave his last public reading some years ago during a National Authors' Week, at Vandervoort Music Hall, in St. Louis, where he was introduced by the beloved William Marion Reedy, of *Spoon River Anthology* fame.

I shall not attempt to mention all the poems and articles by Max Ehrmann that have attracted wide attention throughout the years, nor dwell upon such interludes as the farce, *The Bank Robbery* and *The Plumer,* or other minor writings such as the Scarlet Woman Series.

In 1937 he wrote a *Centennial Ode to Depauw University.* This poem has greatly endeared him to the followers of the Old Gold, as has also a poem entitled *Depauw Revisited.* In 1928 Depauw conferred upon him the degree of Litt. D.

In 1943 his life and writing were the subject of an interesting, broadcast from the studio at Indiana University. His poems are frequently read over the radio from studios all over the country.

I have, perforce, omitted many interesting facts about the life of Max Ehrmann, as well as the titles of some of his works.

I am attempting in a limited time to give only a bare outline of his manifold literary activities. In recent years his writings have been widely syndicated and are familiar to all of you.

Now I have been asked to say a few words to you about Max Ehrmann, the Poet. Though I have known him nearly a quarter of a century, I approach this task in all humility, let me assure you. Furthermore, Mr Ehrmann has expressly asked that what I have to say be brief. Fearful of the lengths to which my friendship for him might carry me, he has begged me not to praise him, but to give merely an outline of his career. I shall respect this wish of his, subject only to the requirements of the topic which has been assigned to me by Dr Albert.

It may be said at the outset, that almost every line that Max Ehrmann ever wrote is intensely poetic because it comes from the soul of a poet, a soul keenly attuned to beauty. Yet it is not in the works which have the conventional structure of poetry that we meet his finest and most moving passages. After all, many people can write lines that can be scanned, and that have rhyme, if need be. But the true poet is the one whose every line of prose gives the illusion of poetry, in whom the poetic vein runs so rich that it pours forth its precious metal in every utterance of his, even in his conversation. This depth of poetic feeling, coupled with a warm, wholesome philosophy which is the result of a lifetime of quiet contemplation of the universe, gave to Max Ehrmann the power and the clear insight with which he interprets himself and his philosophy. His poetry, being the sincere unburdening, of his soul, rather than the mere means of making a living, has the qualities that you and I have come to recognize in the man himself. Let me quote the poem:

A Tradesman and a Poet

'Do these things pay - these poems that you write?'
'Oh! yes, so much I am ashamed
Of my reward, so very great it is.'
'Then tell me why you are so poorly dressed.'
'I did not know that I was poorly dressed.'
'Indeed you are. And think of how you live.
You should have blooming gardens, houses grand,
If your reward is great as you have said.
I understand you live in three small rooms.'
'And that is two too many, I'm afraid.'
You do not travel. Do you travel, sir?'
'Oh! yes, I go each week into the woods,
And often sit upon the river bank.'
'You are not loved by any woman, sir';
And have you any children of your own?'

'I love all women, every child is mine.'

'Come, come, those poems do not pay, I know.'

'Oh! yes, they pay me very well, indeed.

'Then what have you been doing, with the pay

Received? Have you some secret investments?'

'Yes, yes! I have some secret investments.'

'Oh! that is very different. Oh, yes!'

As I had occasion to say recently before a group of students at the college, there are rewards of two basic kinds: the material and the spiritual. Fortunately for us, they often come simultaneously. Not all of us will be richly rewarded for our efforts on the material side; not only shall we not all have deserved it, but we find ourselves unequally equipped with the talents and the resources which win those rewards. On the other hand, not all of us will achieve the spiritual rewards for which we yearn, if by spiritual rewards we insist on meaning the plaudits of society.

In neither case, however, does this mean that we are therefore denied the attainment of the goal of successful living. The urge to seek spiritual rewards rather than material ones has always had certain distinct advantages. When I say this, I am aware that I am harping on an old theme. I know that the materialist, the seeker after *things*, looks with patronizing superiority upon the seeker after spiritual values. Yet the spiritual values, have a staying power that the material things do not seem to have. I am convinced of this faced by long observation of such men as Max Ehrmann. I believe that those who spend their lives in the service of humanity, in the consolation of the weary and the heavy-laden, and in the acquisition of intellectual treasures, achieve a serenity and a satisfaction that are not the lot of the seeker after things. Mere *things*, of whatever sort, can so easily get away from you, whether through taxation, disaster or folly. But intellectual and moral values can never be taken from you, short of insanity or death itself. Max has chosen to fill his head and his heart, rather than to worry about his flimsy pockets.

One of the great services that Max Ehrmann does us, in many of his poems, is to teach us to draw upon the hidden resources of nature and of faith in God, in times of trial. I know no better advice for us, in these times of stress than that found in the poem,

Ere You Lie Down to Sleep

Ere you lie down to sleep in the night, sit still a while and nurse again to life, your gentler self. Forget the restless, noisy spirit of the day, and encourage, to speech the soft voices within you that timidly whisper of the peace of the great, still night; and occasionally look out at the quiet stars. The night will soothe you like a tender mother, folding you against her soft bosom, and hiding you from the harm of the world. Though despised

68

and rejected by men in the light of day, the night will not reject you; and in the still of her soft shadows, you are free. After the day's struggle, there is no freedom like unfettered thoughts, no sound like the music of silence. And though behind you lies a road of dust and heat, and before you the fear of untried paths, in this brief hour you are master of all highways, and the universe nestles in your soul. Therefore, in the night, sit still a while and dream awake, ere you lie down to sleep.

This ability to find renewed strength in quiet and reflexion is one of the salient characteristics of Max Ehrmann, hence one of the most effective themes of his poetic prose. Here is another passage which is a typical expression of his need for renewed courage, but also of his confidence of finding in it in reflexion. Let me quote it:

'*I go inside and close the door; the world has beaten me, and the love has passed out of me. I lock the door and sit thinking of the still woods where I mused in old times, and of the friends and the days that are gone.*

I sit thinking of the gentle old men and women who prowl not about the haunt of trade, thinking of nights of rest and peace, so that the love which has passed out of me may return, and the trembling nerves may grow calm, and the world grow sweet again. Therefore I go inside and close the door.'

Serenity can best be achieved through the creation of a haven of refuge, whether it is an actual, physical one or merely a nook of the inner self into which one can from time to time retire.

But I have not time within these few minutes, to read to you much of the poetry of Max Ehrmann. Nor is it necessary, in order to remind you of his qualities, both as a man and as a poet, to do more than to read *my* favorite passage and, I am sure, that of many of you. In it are the friendliness of this man, his tolerance, his striving for contentment and peace, his innate optimism, his serenity, his self-discipline, his respect for the sacred passion of love, his adaptability to the changing seasons of life, and above all, his staunch faith in the goodness of God. I would give anything that I possess to have written this passage. I would give a great deal to be able to say that I had achieved the serenity of soul that is in its author. I am about to read,

Desiderata

Go placidly amid the noise and the haste, and remember what peace there may be in silence. As far as possible, without surrender, be on good terms with all persons. Speak your truth quietly and clearly; and listen to others, even to the dull and the ignorant; they too have their story. Avoid loud and aggressive persons; they are vexatious to the spirit. If you compare yourself with others, you may become vain or bitter, for always there will be greater and lesser persons than yourself, enjoy your achievements as well as your plans. Keep interested in your career, however humble; it is a real possession in the changing fortunes of time. Exercise caution in your business affairs, for the world is full of trickery. But let this not blind you to what virtue there is; many persons strive for high ideals, and everywhere life is full of heroism. Be yourself. Especially do not feign affection. Neither be cynical about love; for in the face of all aridly and disenchantment, it is as perennial as the grass. Take kindly the counsel of the years, gracefully surrendering the things of youth. Nurture strength of spirit, to shield you in sudden misfortune. But do not distress yourself with dark imaginings. Many fears are born of fatigue and loneliness. Beyond a wholesome discipline be gentle with yourself. You are a child of the universe no less than the trees and the stars; you have a right to be here; And whether or not it is clear to you, no doubt the universe is unfolding as it should. Therefore be at peace with God, whatever you conceive Him to be. And whatever your labor and aspirations, in the noisy confusion of life, keep peace in your soul. With all its sham, drudgery and broken dreams, it is still a beautiful world. Be cheerful. Strive to be happy.

Owing to the time limitations, and because you know it so well, I merely mentioned but did not read to you the earlier poem, *A Prayer*. Whereas in that poem we hear a cry of anguish, a voice calling for reassurance in the flood of doubt, *Desiderata* reveals to us a state of utter confidence in a soul that at last has set foot upon solid ground and can henceforth offer a helping hand to weaker souls who have not yet found the way. Had Max Ehrmann, in all his life, written only *A Prayer* and *Desiderata*, the world would still be eternally in his debt.

Max Ehrmann would not have us gather here merely to acclaim him.

We are here to do him honor because of what we owe him, but also in honoring him, we are doing something that reflects honor upon all of *us*. Terre Haute needs, for her own soul's good, to cherish her gifted children and to reflect upon what they have done to make her just a little better, a little finer than she would have been without them.

MAX EHRMANN

Very Reticent Concerning Honors,

Wins Place Among American Poets

By Olive Inez Downing

Published in the *Indianapolis Star* July 28th 1940

An Author's Study

A just, apportionment of toil's reward should bring
To man the gift of leisure and the tender dream,
The upward look that inward prompts the stars to sing
The wonder of this cosmic thought-pervaded scheme.

Max Ehrmann

Centuries ago trophies of the chase were the awards to the deserving victors, knightly tournaments, heated chariot races, masterly conflicts and ghastly warfare all offered desirable gifts to the winner and conqueror. Jesus came to a wanton world and was crucified by the rabid mob. What did he receive as a memorial? He obtained the greatest trophy securable - the salvation of mankind. Trophies are forever captured by the strongest - spiritually, mentally or physically. Does not the stealthy lioness, with her prey in her mouth, hold it aloft in a proud spirit as she treads to her lair to lay her spoil at the feet of her cubs? Does not the mighty eagle fly majestically to lofty heights to deposit his trophy on the crag of a steep precipice?

In the Terre Haute study of Max Ehrmann, the author, poet and playwright, is seen his trophies of the literary chase in the world of ideal, the securing of which represents years of labor and masterful thought. On the wall by the entrance door hangs one of his trophies - *A Prayer*, a selection that has received worldwide recognition. In circulation it is second to the *Lord's Prayer* and has been translated into 32 languages and dialects - copies printed in millions and in every conceivable form. It was printed in the Congressional Record at Washington.

Inspiration for *Prayer*

The inspiration for writing *A Prayer* arose many years ago. The author was very ill in Columbia, South Carolina, and while recuperating at a hotel there he wrote this gem of thought. He speaks thus of the time:

'One sleepless night I was in and out of my bed more often than usual, I had so little strength in those days. I remember only a few things about that night; one was that it was dark and damp, and another that I could hear the faintest music of a dance across the street from my hotel room.

It seemed to me that all the loneliness of the world crept into my soul, I grew bitter. Bitterness in a man only half alive is no edifying thing, and it is likewise a dangerous thing. Somewhat in this state of mind, as I remember, for my own relief I arose from my bed that damp, dark night, far from home and in a strange country, and wrote A Prayer. *I had written little pieces of prose like this all my life and most of them had gone where this one went - into the wastebasket.'*

But fortunately, this production emanating from the darkness was saved for the alleviation of the disconsolate and distressed. Thus Edwin Markham wrote of it, *'Parts of* A Prayer *are worthy to be graven on granite.'*

Other Brain Children

In his bookcases appear other brain children of his own inimitable conception of life, for Mr Ehrmann is not only a traveller in the world of ideals, but a technician of words, always choosing his phrasing with discrimination. In speaking of his composing he said:

'Sometimes I ponder days on a few lines, chiseling out the words to express the thought I wish to convey. And sitting at my desk a few times it has seemed that something outside of me was guiding my pen.'

Through nearly all Mr Ehrmann's writing, there is this recurring theme:

'There is somewhere an ideal world, maybe only in our own minds, maybe of much vaster extent. Let us try to bring at least

a little of the ideality into our real world - just now a very grim world.'

In his files, was *A Farrago*, his first publication, concerning which he made the following comment:

'It is not really of value, just the work of a boy trying to write.'

However, side by side with it were volumes of great and meritorious worth as *Jesus: A Passion Play* that is conceded by many as a more dramatic and realistic production that the *Oberammergau Passion Play.*

Formidable Array

Near Mr Ehrmann's writing table, on which nearly all his books were written, is a shelf containing the twenty-two books and pamphlets from his pen in a formidable array. Here, too, were most of the twenty-three anthologies containing selections from his writings, among them Star books and Blue Ribbon Books. In leafing through *The Philosophy of Life,* one noticed the comment by the editor, Anderson Baten, Wherein he placed Mr Ehrmann with the philosophers of all ages. On the wall, in front of the writing table, hangs an oval portrait of Mr, Ehrmann's mother - a likeness taken in her sixteenth year. She a gentle, sweet-faced maiden, dressed in the style of her youth, the days following the Civil War. Pointing at the portrait, Mr Ehrmann said:

'That has saved me from the temptation to low deeds.'

Above the mantlepiece was a reproduction of Gilbert Wilson's bust of Max Ehrmann and on the opposite wall hung another likeness with his poem *More than the Dust*, from his *DePauw Centennial Ode*, which contains these, among other significant stanzas:

When you in bitter spirit stamp across the stage
Of the inner theater where so many parts you played,
May there be faith (to soothe your amateurish rage)
That He who wrote the manuscript knows well His trade.

Other unnumbered centuries will come and go,
In man's adventure on this restless grain of dust,
Why all this learning, if we do not strive to know
The Road, the Inn at Night, the Keeper that we trust?

Endeared College Days

While a student at DePauw University Max Ehrmann was editor of the *DePauw Weekly* and on through the years the spirit of the old college has ever remained dear to him. For two years, after graduating from DePauw, he studied philosophy at Harvard University and while there he edited *The Rainbow*, the national magazine of his fraternity, Delta Tau Delta, his *DePauw University Centennial Ode* brought him the degree of Doctor of Letters, another trophy of the literary chase.

In the midst of the seriousness of the interview, Max Ehrmann told us some of the amusing incidents that happened to him in his sojourning in various places. In Jacksonville, Florida, a bookseller tried to induce Mr Ehrmann to purchase a book of his *Jesus: A Passion Play,* saying, '*It is a great book'*. At the *Home of Sick Books*, a second-hand bookshop in Chicago, the dealer tried to sell Mr Ehrmann an autographed volume of his own poems but the signature was not Max Ehrmann's writing, so he autographed the book for the dealer.

Readers Not Convinced

The following is probably the most humorous incident that ever happened to the noted writer. One day he was in the library of the Y.W.C.A. and nearby were two girls searching through the piles of books. Coming upon one of his books they seemed very pleased. Mr Ehmann, wishing to make them happy, stepped forward and said, '*I am Max Ehrmann'*. The girls looked at him in consternation, and one replied, '*What do you take us for! Max Ehrmann died long ago.'* Mr Ehrmann protested that he was not dead, but to no avail, for the second girl said emphatically, '*You are not, he, for we saw his grave at the cemetery this very morning.'* Mr Ehrmann showed them his library card and appealed to some of his friends sitting in the room, but the friends knew him not. What made it more amusing was the fact that the girls would not be convinced. The grave they had seen was that of Mr Ehrmann's father, who also was named Max Ehrmann.

The literary creed of Max Ehrmann is voiced in these words, *'I would rather live plainly and be the author of some bit of chaste prose that should abide amid the perpetual flux than to live luxuriously on the returns of innumerable volumes of merely commercial fiction.'*

Reticent concerning Honors

The author prefers to speak of his work rather than giving personal sketches, and the idea of the trophies of the literary chase is wholly the conception of the writer of this article and data obtained only by questioning and observation, for Mr Ehrmann is very reticent concerning honors won and in no instant is self-laudatory.

On another table lay an album containing photographs, among these was one of the author in his college days - standing very erect in dress suit, high silk hat and white cloves, looking quite dignified and poised. Another photograph of interest was that of Mr Ehrmam, Theodore Dreiser and Robert Heinl taken at Washington. One of Mr Ehrmann's books is *A Life of Paul Dresser,* composer of *On the banks of the Wabash,* the Indiana State song. Paul was the brother of the noted novelist, Theodore Dreiser [who changed his surname], and both were native sons of Terre Haute.

Sought for Justice, Mercy

In all his works, Mr Ehrmann has sought for justice and the intermingling of mercy. Nature lay her beauties before him. He saw the *'changing flecks'* of lights that dotted the sky, the *'pallid gold of summer moons,'* he heard the *'murmur of the meador* [archaic for 'meadow'] *winds, the 'sea whispering in the bosom of the night,'* the *'music that the stars march to so silently and slow'* and sensed the *'pulseless, falling dark.'*

Another trophy that adorned the wall of the author's study was a picture painted by Maxfield Parrish, noted American artist, who represented spring, summer, fall and winter, while the four seasons are vividly illustrated in verse by Max Ehrmann. He is termed a master craftsman. A weaver at life's great loom, he takes the skeins of daily existence and threads then in and out till a picture of exquisite loveliness is revealed. Yet also in his writing is a terrible sense of the stern, hard things of life.

Mystery Unto Myself

'Writing with me is a serious matter,' said Mr Ehrmann. *'there is a spontaneity of thought, but the thought must be filtered through the intellect.'* Continuing with a discussion of his work, he commented:

'Sometimes I am a mystery to myself and out under the stars there, too, I am lost in mystery. From the beauty and profound secrets of the world we get much of our faith. Beyond the night of the present, there must still be another dawn.'

The author's achievements are many, and in a brief account, one can only mention the most outstanding. Among the books in the cases, as we passed along, we saw *Madeline Le Blanc*, *A Fearsome Riddle*, *Who Entereth Here*, *A Virgin's Dream*, *Be Quiet, I'm Talking*, *Faces of Worldly Wisdom*, *Scarlet Sketches* and *Scarlet Series*.

In *Breaking Home Ties* the author told of taking the thought from the painting (by the same name) by the celebrated artist, Hovenden. The selection is a father's rehearsal to his son of the home leaving his youth - the farewell of his mother and father, the sorrowful faces of his two sisters and his grandmother, while even his faithful dog is saddened by his departure. There is voiced the solicitude for his welfare, counsel for his contact with the world both of love and hate - their wise teachings marked his life's course and held him true as steel, with just reward for such an existence.

Most Chaste Volume

Holding up the volume, *The Wife of Marobius*, the author stated, *'This I consider the most chaste production I have ever written.'* Mr Ehrmann has interpreted this play to audiences of wide scope. It has its setting in a luxurious home, a palace with Marobius, a Roman general, as master in his domain. The interior has richly brocaded surroundings, walls embedded with gems, pearls, onyx and jade - a golden dream abode. Marobius hardened by worldly grasping knows only of sensual love while his beautiful wife, Clodia tries to teach him what love really means - its depth, its uplifting power.

As Beatrice led Dante from the darkest pits of Hades to the precipitous heights and pointed out to him the stars in their purity and all of God's firmament, so Clodia led Marobius from worldly passion to the celestial plane of soul devotion. In *Love From Many Angles,* the author states, *'Love places a gauze before the eyes and a commonplace world is changed into a moonlit summer night.'*

In *The Poems of Max Ehrmann* is felt the lure of the unknown, echoes from the past, and voyage on uncharted seas and the serenity of abundant life. The poems are compendiums of rebellion against oppression, hatred and strife, vanity, wickedness and frivolity, also portrayals of peace, chastity and truth - no thought ever tabulated with ephemeral lightness but for eternity. Elbert Hubbard wrote of him:

'It looks to be as if Ehrmann is almost the greatest poet in America.'

The Pittsburgh Gazette Times wrote concerning his poems:

'The most vivid, impassioned, unconventional and individual verse of recent writing. It is real stardust.'

Beloved By Townsmen

Terre Haute is proud of her native son and the murmuring waters of the old Wabash, the gleaming old sycamore through which the candle-lights have twinkled for so many years still lure him with their fascination and ever give new stimulus to the master-poet. Master artist we may call him for his medium is his pen, his colors are his words, and his palette is the whole wide, beautiful world - he choosing from an inexhaustible source.

Mr Ehrmann did not skyrocket to success but earned it by ascending step by step the steep mountain of achievement. He has received international recognition yet he has never become egotistical from the world's acclaim but has gone serenely down the middle road of life. He walks the streets of Terre Haute, a quiet, poetic philosopher, whom his townspeople hold in high esteem.

Diana was the goddess of the chase, a huntress, her name signifying a *'modest, spotless virgin.'* She represented a type of uprightness, purity and great intellect. We can vision our state, as the Indianan Diana of the chase, ever urging, commending and inspiring for the zenith of triumphs, through the years, from the formation of her statehood, she has garnered the conquests of the Hoosier chase into her treasure chest of worthy achievements. So holding the gems of Max Ehrmann's victories, his trophies in her possession, she points proudly to him, saying, *'He is my son.'*

MAX EHRMANN – POET

by George Bicknell

The Caxton, no.4, vol. 11, January 1911

To help another to better bear life's burdens is not to live in vain, and when one builds best for self, he builds best for Eternity. The true artist, in whatever he creates, knows that he must create himself, and few masterpieces were ever carved for the universe intentionally.

Max Ehrmann of Terre Haute, Indiana, modest and unassuming, has come to be recognized as a poet whose productions strike a universal response in human needs and human hopes. Indiana's literary atmosphere has come to be recognized the world over, and around certain centers in Indiana have sprung up certain schools. Terre Haute, the second city in size in the state, is not behind in her individuality in this literary movement; for here seems to have been the birthplace of an ever-widening uplift movement.

The ideals found in Ehrmann's helpful poems were written in hours of his own need of such ideals, and so have answered world needs - for human struggles are universal. Although Ehrmann has lived and struggled in a busy world and has known and felt the real tragedies of the average existence, he has never been willing to make his note anything less than a note of cheer. For years he has been a student of men and of affairs. His schooling has not come altogether from the field of the dreamer, for he is schooled in the world of business, and knows its many struggles.

Ruskin said, *'Young man, never miss seeing the dawn and the sunset, and never see anything between but dreams,'* and Ehrmann has caught this thread and has woven it into the fabric of all his creations. True art should always give the uplift. Nature's final appeal is always upward, and Life must always be lived, however great the tragedies. The need of Human Philosophy is Human Faith - the belief in the ultimate necessity of one's self. And all art is true art which helps to instill this creed in human hearts.

Max Ehrmann, because he lived and struggled and wrote, has helped others to live and struggle and toil. Max, as his friends know him, is one of the common people and believes in their ultimate hopes and aims. He has always written in answer to his own needs and says he has not wrought his poems so much as they have wrought him, and again we are made aware of the fact that people who go out with the intention of doing good never do much good after all, and as teachers we teach least when we think we teach most.

Fifteen years ago, Max, then a youth, wrote out *A Prayer* which he needed to tide himself over what seemed a dark hour. This *Prayer* served its purpose with him and accidently found its way into print. The world needed it, for since that time the world has been willing to pay coin for over a million copies of this *Prayer*. When poetry is vital, it will in some way find its way into the hearts of the people. The *Prayer* was printed, in full, in the December *Caxton*. It is owned and published, in broadside form, by the *Dodge Publishing Company* of New York City.

Many interesting stories have been told relative to this *Prayer*. It has found itself in peculiar conditions and peculiar places. A very beautiful hand-illumined copy of it was stolen from the Indiana Building of the World's Fair at St. Louis. All of the leading dailies throughout the country commented on this incident, but Max's cheerful comment was, *'I am glad it fell into the hands of one who needed it worse than I do.'* A search was made for this copy, but it was never found. This *Prayer* is being used in all walks of life. Judge Leroy B. Crane, of the Court of Special Session of New York, a few years ago received as a gift a copy of this *Prayer*, and at once ordered a supply of them, and to every person in his district who was brought before him he presented one of these *Invocations*. This paragraph from a letter to Mr Ehrmann from the publishers of the *Prayer* is one of many which the author has received - all in the same universal tone.

'Mr Ehrmann: A week or two ago, we were requested by Judge Crane to send a copy of A Prayer *to a man who was supposed to be dying in a hospital, who was very despondent and on the*

verge of taking his life when the Prayer *arrived. The* Prayer *had a wonderful effect on him, and he recovered from his illness and states that he will never be without that* Prayer *no matter where he goes.'* Hundreds of letters attest the helpfulness of this sentiment. These from the lowly walks of life as well as from higher fields: a note from a poor despondent creature, badly spelled and badly written – a bold, free hand from Ellen Terry.

Here is a late story about the *Prayer* from the hand of Curtis L. Mosher, a St. Paul writer: '*On a bitter gray afternoon in winter, when the shadows had lengthened so far as to shut out much of the cheerless light of the day from the magnificent private apartments within, John A. Johnson lent to the cares of a commonwealth the keen and shrewd perception of a well-stored mind and the energy and devotion which lifted him to greatness. I took from an old wallet a well-worn slip of paper and quoted to him the beautiful words of Max Ehrmann's* Prayer. *It was after several hours of trying and arduous labor. Tired and worn the Governor lounged in his leather chair. He sat silent for many minutes and we both gazed out upon the comfortlessness of the dying day.*

'I wish you would repeat those last lines again', *he said.* '*And I come not within sight of the castle of my dreams!*' 'Isn't it magnificent!' *The whole philosophy of a calm, untroubled, gentle, and helpful life breathes out in these simple words,* 'read it all again.' *I repeated the measured phrases and again the silence spread over us. Later we talked, not of greatness and the pomp and circumstances of marching events, but of the common hardships of life and the daily trials and temptations of common men. As we left the huge marble building that commands St. Paul from its remarkable vantage point, John Albert Johnson, plain American, summed up his measure of life in words which it will be hard to forget.* 'It is my conclusion,' *he said,* 'that the bitterness of poverty, the terrible drudgery those who rise from the bottom must experience, the bitter longings and heartaches for the things which we want - want with heart and soul - and always find just beyond us, comprise the best of fire to which far-seeing Providence subjects those who are destined to succeed. And whether real success is possible without this suffering, I doubt.'

Ehrmann is the author of a number of books - most of them in the form of poetry. His poetry contains philosophy especially helpful to struggling needs - a great many of his shorter poems have been widely published in the form of decorated cards, and they hang on the walls of many homes. Among those which the *Dodge Publishing Company* own and have published in beautiful form are:

Who Entereth Here, You Who Come at Evening, Love Some One, Evening Song, The Greater Heroism, The House of Fortune, An Easter Prayer and *An Artist's Prayer.*

Through the kindness of the *Dodge Publishing Company*, I am able to reproduce some of these here.

The Greater Heroism

Work as if thy task were made for thee;
Be strong as if thou hadst courage,
And charitable as if thou hadst been rewarded;
Remain poor if riches are dishonorable,
And carry poverty with the dignity of virtue.
When others dine sumptuously, eat thy crust;
Let love be thy guide and justice thy God -
Not for thyself alone, but for all men.
Pursuing these things thou wilt be misjudged
And, in the gloaming of thy days, forgotten;
Then, uncomplaining, lie thou down at even,
Cheered by the love in thy heart,
And by the full-grown soul of thy charity;
Then hast thou won the heroic battle,
Yet not stained the sweet earth with blood;
But in the garden of love and sacrifice,
Hast thou planted serenely growing flowers,
That shall still blow when thou dost slumber
In the shadow-land of dreamless sleep.

The House of Fortune

How heartless is the strife of men to enter the doorway of the house of fortune. But the great triumph is to stand cheerfully outside and serve, though the coveted doorway open ever and anon to them of lesser virtue, and to grow old meanwhile, with face turned toward the golden west, watching the last sunset, loving, hoping, and believing still, and through the mist of the world, to see yet the god of your youth, but grown gentler and more compassionate, as you yourself are gentler and more compassionate. After all, is not this to have entered the doorway, and to have dwelt in the house of fortune?

Love Some One

Love someone - in God's name love someone - for this is the bread of the inner life, without which a part of you will starve and die; and though you feel you must be stern, even hard, in your life of affairs, make for yourself at least a little corner, somewhere in the great world, where you may unbosom and be kind.

An Artist's Prayer

Lord God, thou who dost paint with magic touch
The curtains of the soft and silent night,
This gift I ask, that o'er whatever cloth
My brush may glide, now to and fro and 'round,
There will come that which ever pleases thee.
Help me to make the things that beauty hold
Amid these veering lines and diverse shades,
That cheer will bring to sad and solemn men
And tired women in their dreary haunts,
That youth will not forget on highways hard
With troubled years, when somber night is on,
And when no kindly light leads through the way,
That joy and love may dawn like newborn days
In hearts where long the chambers have been dark.
Let lowly life and dusty, daily toil
Come near me evermore and day by day,
That I forget not them that still are kind
Though tried by years of unrequited toil,
Alas! and sometimes want and age and pain.
Let me not love my pictures more than men,
Nor follow the wild lead of some mad dream,
Nor see myself as if above the crowd

Commanding that they all shall bow their heads;
Instead, with kindly heart and gentle hand
And smiles upon my face, let me serve them
Whose muscles ache at evening's twilight fall
While mine in comfort still are fresh and strong.
May all these be not empty, idle words,
But all the burden of my life's sweet task.
And when thou seest that my work is done,
Let me feel thy soft evening shadows fall
As when I climbed into my nursery bed
With childish faith in time's old long ago;
And let the kiss of peace lie on my lips.

MAX EHRMANN

By George Bicknell

Written for *Appleton's Cyclopedia of American Biography* circa 1917, unpublished, DePauw University Archives

An appreciation of an author must deal with his writings, for they represent what is going on inside him.

Some years have passed since I wrote a magazine article about Max Ehrmann. In that article I treated him as a moralist. Since them he has done that which makes him an artist – an artist leagues ahead of his former character of moralist.

A philosophical statement of Max Ehrmann as a moralist would be something like the following. His thinking is a mixture of the philosophy of Jesus and Nietzsche. He believes in love and service, as taught by Jesus. But he also believes, with Nietzsche, that the evolution of man must not be retarded. Once he said to me, *'What if the monkeys had adopted Christianity'* And then he showed that if the ethics of Jesus - love and service - had taken hold of prehistoric animals, man would never have been developed. It was selfishness that made the struggle for existence and the consequent survival of the fittest - man. Thus far he is with Nietzsche. But he believes that the process of evolution can continue now by *'artificial selection'*, coupled with love and service as taught by Jesus. The first step in this direction he has pointed out over and over again is to prevent the breeding of defectives.

If Mr Ehrmann's earlier books - especially *Breaking Home Ties* and the collected *Poems* - are read in the light of this ethical viewpoint they will be better understood. All through the earlier productions, one finds the selfish, grinding world realistically pictured; and just so pictured also one finds the vision of a greater destiny for man.

Since 1911 Max Ehrmann has produced three books which have given him real importance as an artist. In the autumn of that year appeared *The Wife of Marobius,* a play of only three characters. It is as finely done as a piece of lace, of which, indeed, it reminded some critics. It has the simplicity and dignity of things made by the ancient Greeks. J. William Lloyd, in *The New Review*, likened it to a Greek temple. Mr William Faversham, the well-known actor, wrote of it,

O gracious me, how I should like to play it! Does one dare put it on the stage? I picked it up and started to read it, and I never stopped. Then I read it over again, and in my mind, I stage-managed and produced it. Really, it is full of great, great chances; but dare one do it on the public stage?'

Writing in *The Poetry Review* – London, Mr Harrold Hoare, the editor, said of *The Wife of Marobius* 'There is *beauty and color in the setting, charm in the rhythmic music of the lines, and the grip of real human emotion.'*

Pointing out the artistic worth of the lace weaving in words of this play, Vandervoort Sloan says in *The Drama*,

'It treats with great beauty the theme of the wife who loves beauty of soul and the husband who loves beauty of body. It is a drama of psychology and sex finely done, a play which has received more deserved admiration in England than here at home. Three qualities are marked in this early drama - a fine and sure sense of technique, a subtle understanding of the feminine mind, reminding one a little of Fiona Macleod, and a noble feeling for beauty at once sensuous and moral. The scene is laid in pre-christian days in Rome, and one is carried back to that period as completely as he is in the dramatization Mr Ehrmann later made of the story of Christ.'

The Wife of Marobius showed that Max Ehrmann was really an artist. There are lines in this play made of threads of gold. It is a daring treatment of the situation that presents itself when there is a conflict between love of the spirit and love of the flesh.

Some critics, acknowledging the beauty and daring of this play, regretted that its author had not the talent to produce a large piece with a greater number of characters and acts. As stated before, *The Wife of Marobius* had only three characters.

As if irritated by such criticism, Mr Ehrmann next produced *Jesus: A Passion Play*. This play has five big, sets, several mobs and fifty-two speaking parts, at least thirty of whom are highly individualized characters. Jesus is treated as a man and not a God. But the author's interest in this thesis gives way, as the play procedes, to his desire to write powerful and beautiful things. Here are two hundred and eighty-two pages of strain, noise and excitement. Here is a fierce conflict between powerful reality and exaulted idealism. The people have not read Max Ehrmann. Excepting *A Prayer* they have no great acquaintance with his work. This is not true because his work has no relation to life; but because of that very reason, it treats of life profoundly. His work is not a substitute for candy or cigars. Coteries of aesthetes read him; also professors, artists and writers. (I do not know any other modern American author who has been so praised by writers). Writing of *Jesus: A Passion Play*, Jack London, that lover of brute force, said,

'More than anything else, what I like about it is its unrelenting reality and brass-tactism. From beginning to end it is real. It is what surely might have happened.'

Rupert Hughes, the well-known novelist, said of *Jesus: A Passion Play*,

'The foundation is clear cold logic and a finely reached plausibility. The spirit is one of heart-breaking beauty. I don't know when I have read anything of more pitiful appeal than the apostrophe of Joseph of Arimathea to the memory of Jesus. There is a kind of noble agony throughout the play that puts it high among the big tragedies.'

98

And Basil King, the novelist, wrote among other things of this play *'I could not read the book otherwise than carefully since the presentation is as remarkable and the interest so intense. I wish I could give anything like an idea of the impression the work has made on me. The vivid and yet poetic realism brings it before the eyes of the mind to a degree which I cannot remember having seen equalled elsewhere'.* Zangwill, wrote in London, among other things, *'I have enjoyed many an artistic moment in this interpretation. I wish indeed we could have on the stage such symphonic effects and such poetic entrancements. I think such work as this must ultimately educate the world in the true inwardness of the Christian saga.'*

High praise, all this, from men who are themselves craftsmen in words! And page after page could be added of what writers and critics of different degrees of merit have written in different times and places about this play.

And in *Jesus: A Passion Play* Max Ehrmann commits his real, and I believe only important, artistic sin. There is an over-packing of the pages with details. *The Wife of Marobius* is entirely free from this. But in most of his work there is often the want of courage to omit. On the other hand, *Jesus: A Passion Play* is so complete a conception on the last three days of the life of Jesus, that whoever in the future treats of this period cannot afford to overlook this big piece of work.

The art in Mr Ehrmann's last play *David and Bathsheba*, is more chaste than in *Jesus*. Vandervoort Sloan, writing in the November 1917 number of *The Drama* (where the play first appeared) says, '*His finest achievement up to the present is his play* David and Bathsheba.'

One achievement of this latest play is the language, not an archaic imitation, but a living speech, breathing the spirit of Hebraic days in all its vivid oriental beauty, yet never losing the flexibility of real speech, varied from character to character, and maintaining at the same time a beauty of imagery and diction which the followers of free verse forms may study to advantage. Mr Ehrmann is a rare combination of high moral purpose, sound health, and great sensitiveness to sensuous beauty. In *David and Bathsheba*, this alignment finds peculiarly harmonious material. At unity with his subject matter, the author is free to give himself over to its effective expression. The result is a drama of a technique remarkable in poetic or oriental drama, a drama which, in spite of the cumbering associations of its story, contains the humor and tragedy of life and produces a single impression of ever mounting passion and spiritual power.

Throughout the retelling of this old story, he has portrayed the people who figured in it with a vividness unusual in verse-dramas, and with, a remarkable emotional as well as intellectual understanding of the period.' [unattributed]

Max Ehrmann sits at his table writing much as a composer sits at his piano composing. He has a sensitive ear. He hammers out his work on an anvil of steel. The music of his style in the plays is infectious. It is this piano-forte method of composition that no doubt accounts for some of its finest effects.

While many other writers hurriedly produced book after book, one and sometimes two a year of sickly romantic character, Max Ehrmann writes on big themes, takes his time, and labors long, to bring real treasures to that smaller circle of lovers of beautiful creations, never doubting that he is steering his ship toward the harbor of things remembered - at any rate, remembered for a little while.

In conclusion, I shall quote again Mr Sloan's article in *The Drama*, for it is the most recent, and truly represents this author. '[Here] *is a persistent note of fine friendliness, of pervading humanness. With such a basis that it is small wonder that he is an altruist, a believer in idealistic politics, in the speedy coming of a rich brotherhood among the world peoples who in our present crisis promise so little to such a consummation.*'

Let me add that piece of prose that shows what manner of man this author is - at any rate shows his aspirations - that piece of prose which brought him a kind of fame, for it has been printed into the millions of copies, translated, and is known almost the world over - *A Prayer*.

MAX EHRMANN

By J. Vandervoort Sloan

The Drama: A Quarterly Review Devoted to the Drama, No.
28, November 1917

The author of *David and Bathsheba,* Max Ehrmann,
suffered the usual trials and tribulations of the young
writer before he really arrived. He, however, went on
his way disregarding the lack of appreciation which is
the common lot and often the undoing of the writer
who   is   serving   his   novitiate.   Whatever
disappointment he may have felt at least he did not
express in his writings.

Mr Ehrmann was   graduated   from   De   Pauw
University in 1893. He was then twenty-one years old.
What his philosophizing, his happiness, his suffering
and his viewpoint of life were during and preceding
his college days, he alone knows. One judges from his
poems to follow that the years were full of
restlessness. Booth Tarkington has told in a measure
of the joys and sorrows of the late 'teens, those years
when a boy who thinks - and many, doubtless, who
do not - feels that he is *'misunderstood'* and as a matter
of fact he usually is.

The musings and meditations of Mr Ehrmann led

him to take up the study of philosophy during the years immediately following his graduation from De Pauw. While he was studying law, he also worked under Professors Royce, Palmer and Munsterberg at Harvard. The year that Max Ehrmann finished his Harvard courses his first book was published. This was in 1898; and the volume, a collection of prose stories and sketches, was called *A Farrago*. He returned this same year to his home in Terre Haute and took up the practice of law, which he continued for several years. When he was twenty-six years old, already locally well known as a thinker and reformer in public questions, Mr Ehrmann was asked to be candidate for state senator, a doubtful honor which he declined.

During these years he was giving much of his time to writing, his inclination fostered, no doubt, by his Cambridge associations. Mr Ehrman's first published novel, *The Mystery of Madeleine Le Blanc*, appeared in 1900. His next, and up to the present the last novel written by him, was entitled *A Fearsome Riddle*, and came out the following year. Nothing more was published after that until 1905, when he brought forth a poem in blank verse, *Breaking Home Ties*, suggested by the familiar Hovenden picture of the same title. With this Mr Ehrmann had his first real success; now after twelve years, there is still a demand for the book. However, as yet he had created no work of real significance.

A Prayer, published in 1906, gave him genuine popular fame. The inspiration for this was very likely found in the well-known prayer of Robert Louis Stevenson; but as Mr Ehrmann's *Prayer* has had a much greater circulation than the one written by R.L.S., and as it is quite as beautiful, it merits consideration. More than a million copies of *A Prayer* have been sold.

Excepting the *Lord's Prayer*, no prayer ever published in the English language has been so widely circulated as *A Prayer*, written by the poet-playwright, Max Ehrmann. It has been printed in every conceivable form, in copies numbering into the millions. It has been inserted into the Congressional Record at Washington. It has been often translated and set to music. It has been stolen from public buildings, pirated, modified and plagiarized, found on the bodies of suicides, the last solace of condemned criminals, the daily lesson of millions of school children, the cherished possession alike of the Fifth Avenue millionaires and the Bowery poor of many great cities. Thousands of persons who never go inside a church read and love it. It is the prayer universal because work is its creed and love its religion.

Nearly a score of years ago Max Ehrmann, the poet-playwright, lay ill in Columbia, South Carolina, where he had gone to get well or to die. There are persons at Columbia who still remember Max Ehrmann venturing slowly forth from his hotel once or twice a week, well wrapped up and leaning heavily on a cane. In a letter to a friend written some years later, the poet told how he came to write *A Prayer:*

'One sleepless night it seemed I was in and out of my bed more than usual. I had so little strength in those days. I remember only a few things about that night, one that it was dark and damp, and another, that I could hear the faint music of a dance across the street from my room. It seemed to me that all the loneliness of the world crept into my soul. I grew bitter. Bitterness in a man only half alive is certainly no edifying thing. And it is likewise a very dangerous thing. Somewhat in this state of mind, as I remember, for my own relief, I arose from my bed that damp, dark night, far from home, in a strange and friendless country, and wrote A Prayer. *Dear me! as I remember, I had written little pieces of prose like this all my life, and most of them had gone where this one went, into the wastebasket.'*

A Prayer

'Let me do my work each day; and if the darkened hours of despair overcome me, may I not forget the strength that comforted me in the desolation of other times. May I still remember the bright hours that found me walking over the silent hills of my childhood, or dreaming on the margin of the quiet river, when a light glowed within me, and I promised my early God to have courage amid the tempests of the changing years. Spare me from bitterness and from the sharp passions of

unguarded moments. May I not forget that poverty and riches are of the spirit. Though the world know me not, may my thoughts and actions be such as shall keep me friendly with myself. Lift my eyes from the earth, and let me not forget the uses of the stars. Forbid that I should judge others lest I condemn myself. Let me not follow the clamor of the world, but walk calmly in my path. Give me a few friends who will love me for what I am; and keep ever burning before my vagrant steps the kindly light of hope. And though age and infirmity overtake me, and I come not within sight of the castle of my dreams, teach me still to be thankful for life, and for time's olden memories that are good and sweet; and may the evening's twilight find me gentle still.'

Ehrmann's first drama, *The Wife of Marobius*, was published in 1911, a one-act play that treats with great beauty the theme of the wife who loves beauty of soul and the husband who loves beauty of body. It is a drama of psychology and sex finely done, a play which has received more deserved admiration in England than here at home. With the little theatres constantly crying for new material of beauty, it is strange that this exquisitely chiseled play has never been produced. Three qualities are marked in this early drama - a fine and sure sense of technique, a subtle understanding of the feminine mind, reminding one a little of Fiona Macleod, and a noble feeling for beauty at once sensuous and moral. The scene is laid in pre-christian days in Rome, and one is carried back to that period as completely as he is in the dramatization Mr Ehrmann later made of the story of Christ.

He has called this *Jesus: A Passion Play*. As in *The Wife of Marobius*, there is fine sense of atmosphere. *The New Testament* is drama which was well handled by those who wrote it. The attempts to make it more dramatic have never been wholly successful. Maeterlinck in *Mary Magdalene*; Paul Heyse in *Maria von Magdala*, and the Grand Duke Constantine of Russia in his *King of the Jews* have retold the familiar episodes of the life of Jesus as if each felt that he was improving on the original. Maurice Browne, who wrote another version called *The King of the Jews*, and Charles Rann Kennedy in *The Terrible Meek* attempted by introducing cockney dialect to make realistically dramatic the simply written drama as set forth by Matthew, Mark, Luke and John. The results were interesting, but not wholly satisfying, for while the immediate dramatic effect was striking, the later final impression was weakened. Symbol, especially religious symbol of the long ago, needs the chaste atmosphere of the remote if it is to give its spiritual message unclouded. Mr Ehrmann has been somewhat more successful in retaining the feeling of the period than any of his contemporaries, but his play of the life of Jesus, the money changers in the Temple, and the Magdalene is not his best work. One feels the author's sincerity, his earnest effort to revitalize the Christ story in terms, not of conventional belief, but of simple human tragedy and simple human faith which looks through the tragedy for the old heart belief and the old heart inspiration, now to so many lost in the religious brocade of doctrine. Yet even Mr Ehrmann loses his technique through the meshes of the Bible material and, in spite of many telling scenes, fails to give the simple totality and nobility of the original.

His finest achievement up to the present is his play *David and Bathsheba*. In this he has as in *Jesus* written in the spirit and vernacular of the time, and the result is a lyric play almost as lovely as its inspiration.

One achievement of this latest play is the language, not an archaic imitation, but a living speech, breathing the spirit of Hebraic days in all its vivid oriental beauty, yet never losing the flexibility of real speech, varied from character to character, and maintaining at the same time a beauty of imagery and diction which the followers of free verse forms may study to advantage. Mr Ehrmann is a rare combination of high moral purpose, sound health, and great sensitiveness to sensuous beauty. In *David and Bathsheba* this alignment finds peculiarly harmonious material. At unity with his subject matter the author is free to give himself over to its effective expression. The result is a drama of a technique remarkable in poetic or oriental drama, a drama which, in spite of the cumbering associations of its story, contains the humor and tragedy of life and produces a single impression of ever mounting passion and spiritual power.

Throughout the retelling of this old story he has portrayed the people who figured in it with a vividness unusual in verse-drama, and with a remarkably emotional as well as intellectual understanding of the period. As a playwright, as a philosopher, and as a poet Mr Ehrmann's work suggests '*Year's at the spring*', because the spark within tells him that '*God's in his Heaven, All's right with the world.*' This element in his work has given it an appeal to a wide public usually not addicted to literature of a type as worthwhile as that which this author presents. Coupled with this quality, perhaps necessarily for one of his mettle, is a persistent note of fine friendliness, of pervading humanness. With such a basis it is small wonder that he is an altruist, a believer in idealistic politics, in the speedy coming of a rich brotherhood among the world peoples who in our present crisis promise so little to such a consummation. A prose poem representing a portion of this attitude is interesting as a partial revelation of the author:

> '*Love some one - in God's name love some one -*
> *for this is the bread of the inner life, without which*
> *a part of you will starve and die; and though you feel*
> *you must be stern, even hard, in your life of affairs,*
> *make for yourself at least a little corner, somewhere*
> *in the great world, where you may unbosom and be*
> *kind.*'

BELOVED DEAD

Published in *Tony's Scrap Book,* 1911-12 edition.

Spoken by Max Ehrmann at the funeral services of a friend.

How peaceful lie the dead! Why do we weep, since they mourn not? Well-beaten is the path they take into the great unknown. We follow them a little way, till dusk to darkness turns, then parting wave farewell. We do not know what is at their journey's end. But as we trust the sun will rise, so we trust the mystery of life and death will be explained to us sometime and we shall be content... Farewell, thou gentle sleeper – we will not say forever, but for a few brief suns and moons, when we also shall pass out of the beautiful earth. We know not with what authority, but the ever-dawning, deathless hope of all the ages tells us that somehow we shall know thee again. Art thou, in some mystical way, already seated near the Helmsman of the universe, in wonder cruising some celestial sea of worlds? If all is not over with thee, does thou with kindly memory still look upon our little earth? And wilt thou sometimes think of us remembering happy hours we spent together in this radiant sun-kissed world? Thus shall we not be all alone; for often thou wilt come to us, and we shall see thee by our side, and in the stillness hear thy voice. O speak to us in spirit whispers when sorrow bears us down! Thy placid face now tells us not to grieve, for peace is thine. Farewell, thou gentle sleeper. How still thou art!

PROMOTIONAL COMMENTS

FROM 1906 to 1951

Book Cover Quotes for

A Prayer and other Selections, published in 1906

What our country thinks of Max Ehrmann:

North

'The volume is a reflection of Max Ehrmann, the man, a personage well worth knowing and loving, and it should make him many friends. Those who read this delightful volume will recognise the true poet and accord a high place among the rare few gifted with the poet's art.'

Grand Rapids Herald

'A book of great power, praising with lyric beauty the gentler things of life; and plunging the knife of keen criticism into the barbarities of our modern life.'

Saginaw Evening News

South

'It is as the philanthropist of the printed page that Max Ehrmann excels. Through the poems run the high desire to rid the human heart of burdens.'

Charlesworth, South Carolina, *News Courier*

'Strong in feeling, original in conception, and clear in expression. They raise a protest against the grinding down of the poor, the idleness of the rich, the fever of the commercial world; against hypocrisy, greed, artificiality.'

New Orleans Picayune

East

'Previous volumes of Max Ehrmann's verse have achieved a popularity which is likely to be sustained… Powerfully and convincingly written.'

Philadelphia Press

'This is a thoughtful book for thoughtful people. There is much beauty in the thoughts and much spirituality. Among so many beautiful things it is hard to choose – beautiful enough to be repeated frequently as collects are repeated in churches.'

Brooklyn Citizen

West

'Once read they will be read over and over again. They are full of love and wonder of God's world, of sweetness and light. These are helpful, hopeful, optimistic, worthy to be illuminated and hung on the wall for daily companionship. But the most exquisite things in the book are not in rhyme but in prose, a glorified prose that is truly poetry.'

Leavenworth Times

Book Cover Quotes for

The Wife of Marobius and other plays,

published in 1911

'His is poetry exquisite, pure literature, passion superb, a setting sensuous and colourful, conveying a moral the most advanced, modern, heroic, yet true for the womanhood of all times.'

The New Review

'In understanding the lives of men and women and in his deep insight into the human heart, Max Ehrmann has won a notable place among American writers... a dignity of style, a notable eloquence of expression, a dramatic intensity that are tremendously compelling.'

Buffalo Courier

'A distinct contribution to American dramatic literature. A subtle understanding of the feminine mind and a noble feeling for beauty at once sensuous and moral.'

Drama Magazine

***

Book Cover Quotes on

Desiderata

First published in 1927

(excepts from letters to Mrs Max Ehrmann, a.k.a.
Bertha Pratt King)

'This a very moving statement. A very profound wisdom shines through these sentences which could not fail to affect anyone who reads them.'

Nathan Pusey, President of Harvard University

'Thanks you for this fine scroll of sound advice. I am going to have it framed for my office wall.'

Estes Kefauver, US Senator

'Your husband's wonderful Desiderata*! It is beautiful and I shall keep it near at hand so that I many often reread it.'*

Judge Sherman Minton, US Supreme Court

'The fine spirit and the words of wisdom will be an inspiration to me, I assure you.'

Leverett Saltonstall, US Senator

'This inspiring and solacing philosophy! Time again I have found its precept applicable to the problems of my own life and to those of others. I shall draw upon it frequently in the future.'

Governor Frank Lausche, Ohio

'How wise your distinguished husband was! The Desiderata *is like reading from the proverbs. Nothing moved me more than the statement* 'Do not feign affection. Neither be cynical about love; for in the face of all aridity and disenchantment, it is as perennial as the grass'. *Thank you so very, very much.'*

Bishop G Bromley Oxnam

'Your husband made a real contribution to world literature and of permanent value when he composed it. I have given it to many and many a person.'

Dr. Merrill Moore, Boston

***

Book Cover Quotes for
The Poems of Max Ehrmann,
Edited by Bertha Pratt King, 1948

'These poems have a high spiritual quality – so much thought and feeling, so much dignity, so much simplicity of feeling. He had a rare social vision. His passionate humanism flames in many vivid lines.'

Claude Bowers

'Max Ehrmann has been about the world, looking with a clear eye, and tells about it with a sharp pen... These poems are honest and straight-forward and are written by a man who has a grasp of literature and a power of expression.'

Sinclair Lewis

'One rises from a perusal of these pages conscious of having communed with one of the world's teachers, if not prophets.'

Brooklyn Citizen

'Here is much food for thought and inspiration for the soul... depth of spirit, calm repose and peaceful unity of life. Truly we need to pause in the turmoil of life for such a feast. A distinctly unique contribution to the literature of America. He has enriched and inspired our culture.'

O.L. Bockstahler, Indiana University

'When a man as creative and sensitive as Max Ehrmann will come to terms with the problems before us all, his contribution is important. Here is some thinking in historic mold.'

Dr. Preston Bradley, Chicago

'A Prayer has simplicity, majesty, tenderness. The words are worthy to be engraved on granite.'

Edwin Markham

'Above all else he is a student of the deep problems of life… a philosophy of awareness and reconsideration of the real values of life. His road to happiness is strangely alluring.'

Indianapolis Star

***

Book Cover Blurb for

Max Ehrmann: A Poet's Life
by Bertha Pratt King, 1951

'Any biography of Max Ehrmann would be that of the inner life for above all else he was deeply concerned with the spiritual meanings of life, the social problems of the day and how to live in a distracted world.

Max Ehrmann was not an ivory tower philosopher. The pattern of his life was admirable. He practised law for several years, was a deputy prosecuting attorney and later connected to the business world for many years. His writings give counsel for wise living and inspiring reflections on life. He foresaw the problems of today, the swift changes from the old certainties to modern doubts and fears. His poems are a stirring appeal for men and women to meet their social responsibilities. His well-known Desiderata *and* A Prayer *will long remain his bequest for those who search for some helpful philosophy for living.'*

***

ABOUT THE EDITOR

Tim Dalgleish is the author of two volumes of poetry *The Stones of Mithras* and *Penumbra*, numerous plays and a book on acting called *Playing Macbeth: An Actor's Journey into the Role* (called by reviewers 'A thrilling journey' and a 'Fantastic insider's view'). As an actor he has worked with theatre companies from RAT Theatre to Voices of the Holocaust.

He played Snout in *A Midsummer Night's Dream* as part of the RSC's Open Stages programme and was the lead in *Macbeth* for the Open Theatre Group. He has appeared briefly in several feature films, the most recent being the British-Muslim comedy *Finding Fatimah* and the (soon to be released) gangster movie *Milk and Honey*, he was also in the short film *Imagine* which received Special Mention at the Marbella International Film Festival.

His third collection of essays, *The Three Hearts of the Octopus* was recently published and follows on from two previous collections, *The Purple Rose* and *Orwell, Two Guinea Pigs, A Cat and A Goat*. He regularly narrates audio books, the latest being: *Hamelin's Child* by DJ Bennet and *After Dunkirk: D-Day and How We Planned the Second Front* by Major John Dalgleish (his great uncle). More information at www.lookingfortim.com.

ALSO BY TIM DALGLEISH

Non-Fiction

Scotland before Scotland

Lifting it off the Page

The Guerilla Philosopher

Playing Macbeth: An Actor's Journey into the Role

Poetry

Reflections from Mirror City (anthology)

The Stones of Mithras

Penumbra

Plays

The Last Days of Adam

The Life and Theatre of Antonin Artaud

Essays

The Purple Rose and other essays

Orwell, Two Guinea Pigs, A Cat and A Goat and other essays

The Three Hearts of the Octopus

Editor

The Rose by WB Yeats

Dracula's Guest by Bram Stoker

The Ballad of Reading Gaol with Humanitad by Oscar Wilde

After Dunkirk by Major John Dalgleish